Surviving

on

BROKEN

PIECES

Lynda Joice

Strive Publishing

ISBN-13: 978-0-9786001-5-0

Edited/formatted by Shonell Bacon

Cover designed by Nirkri

DEDICATION

This book is dedicated to the memories of my father Deacon Levoy E. Taylor and my grandfathers, Rev. Percy Fennell and Mr. Ernest L. Taylor.

Thank you for laying my foundation to becoming a living vessel.

CONTENTS

ACKNOWLEDGMENTS

I would like to thank my children Taressa Sanders and Mack D. Sanders. You both always have my back. You both are very supportive. I picked two wonderful seeds to mother. You are my jewels. Keep shining.

Thank you, Shawn Lawrimore, Stephanie Johnson, Monique Hills, Xavier Harrison, Mother Hines, Mychal Harris, and Deborah Hodges for your prayers and for believing in my gift to write and never waver. I would like to acknowledge my mother Ruth Taylor and my extended family for your love and all of your support. Thank you.

INTRODUCTION
We All Need a Survival Kit

There are so many twists and turns in the roads we travel on our life journey. On any road, we'll find traffic lights, stop signs, potholes, crossroads, and other road blocks. The journey may even cause individuals to pass through construction sites, traffic or, even worst, an accident that may be fatal. Wherever the trail leads, the best way to conquer anything is to believe and focus on moving forward. Everyone's journey is different. Excel at being the best you that you can be.

Declare that you have a made-up mind no matter how circumstances look or even how you might feel while buried in those circumstances. Tell yourself daily that you love yourself and that you are important to yourself. I believe in every situation there is a lesson to be learned. Distractions that try to eat at emotions, try to steal finances, attack peace, torment the mind, and even try to bruise the soul do not define the great person inside of you. They are simply road blockers. You might think the best course of action is to fight back, but that's not always applicable.

I have been on many bridges during a dark moment in my life, and I would want to drive off those bridges, too. However, I realized that committing suicide would be selfish as others would be unfairly inflicted by such a traumatic loss. I often talk to myself and say, "Self, I can get through anything." Tell yourself the same thing—that you can overcome anything. Believe it. Put Christ in your vehicle. Let Him take the wheel. In our weaknesses, Christ is always stronger than our circumstances. Continue to hold fast and be unmovable. Plant your feet on the solid rock. Tell yourself that you are like a palm tree planted on a sure foundation. Yes, talk to yourself out loud. I remember being taught that even through the worst of storms, palm trees will bend down very low to the ground, but they never break! Positive self-talks are essential. They are a great gift to give to yourself. Even if you have to cry through a dark time, move forward while shedding the tears. Crying is cleansing and very therapeutic. Not to mention flowers cannot grow without water.

I strongly believe that everyone has a story to tell, even if the person may not know how to articulate it. Our stories demonstrate how we overcome. We overcome by the words of our testimonies. Speak life over yourself. Conquering may not happen overnight.

Sometimes, we may have to be our own cheerleaders and shout that it is possible to SURVIVE this journey. Begin to peel off the deadness that could have attached on. And one of the best attributes to have first is a made-up mind of determination. You are a soldier! Fight on! Fight!

Many days, I have physical challenges. I also used to feel stuck, but I am far from being a quitter. I know there is light at the end of every tunnel. But, baby, I had to fight often for my life. I learned that I was fearfully and wonderfully made. I had to learn how to shut down those negative, taunting thoughts. I knew discouragement only came to *encourage* my demise. What would get me sometimes is I only saw darkness. But I had to tell myself to believe no matter what. No matter how heavy it appeared. I kept moving forward and believing that nothing was permanent and that things were going to be better for me.

Struggles are real. Pain can hurt and can cut deeply. Disappointments are never planned. They aren't always deserved and can be rather brutal. When these culprits are bouncing around you, befriend patience and active outlets to keep you out of a mental dark place. There could be so much stress that airways become clogged, so much that lungs collapse. Anxiety, depression, and panic attacks will sing your melody. Fight on! You got this!

I believe surviving is a choice that we all can make. Committing suicide is also a choice. It is a choice to quit and die. Continuing to live is also a choice. A choice to move on and be a winner. Joy and peace are obtainable if you only believe. Work through pain, beat odds, and travail to be set free emotionally, physically, and mentally. Freedom is your birthright. You are more than a conqueror! With the right tools, you can fight and survive through the "Hunger Games" of life. Dig inside, reach for your dreams. I guarantee you, honey, what you need is inside of you. Believe in you. It is not time to wear grave clothes. Fight on!

Just like seasons change, life has cycles that also change. Life has four seasons: winter, spring, summer, and fall. Just remember after fall and winter, spring and summer always show up. Learning how to hold on is the craft given by God the Father. Don't die in the winter. Don't die in that cold, lonely, dark, dry, dead place. Fight until summer comes and then, baby, go swimming in a pool of joy, peace, and laughter. Or take a long walk on the beach where there is *Sonshine*. Summer is coming if you endure and persevere.

Not once did I say a journey was pain free. Not once did I say there never would be days that you won't feel like quitting. Do not QUIT! Never isolate yourself from others. What you may be facing, is a caterpillar experience that has the potential to become a butterfly. Do not die in the winter. Someone needs to hear your testimony of how you survived. And that first someone is you. Speak life into your dead situations. You are on your way out. Just believe it even if you can't see it.

FORGIVENESS IN LIFE IS A NECESSITY.

Forgiveness is a liberating and a wonderful piece of art to behold. It is a beautiful piece of art created to bring abundant peace to you. Nevertheless, some have learned not to forgive because of lack of trust or repeated offenses. Letting go of a hurt can make it challenging to forget, to move on, and to forgive. Individuals may pick up not learning to forgive by the environment that they grew up in. Or they have witnessed the dynamics of a brutal offense that has inflicted them physically, mentally, and emotionally. That behavior can usher a seed of anger, rage, and even hatred. Lack of forgiveness can also create other behaviors that will control a life.

Exercising forgiveness can be accomplished without receiving an apology. In other words, an individual doesn't have to wait until a person verbally apologizes to give forgiveness. Forgiveness can be an intentional act demonstrated from the heart. It's knowingly releasing an offense. It begins with saying that the person is forgiven. Just forgive because for real it is unhealthy to hold venom inside. Lack of forgiveness carries so many pesticides that eat at emotions, destroy organs, and may clog a life.

My roller coaster ride of life has had several teachable moments demonstrating how I have been kept and carried through the good, bad, and sometimes ugly. Forgiving was essential for me. Without it, I had become someone inside that I wasn't meant to be. Baby, that stranger came from a tree that had roots.

Rejection was not my friend, but she walked with me for a great portion of my life. I didn't want to feel rejected. And I did not welcome the hold it had on me. I didn't like that this unwanted creature followed me day after day after day. Years ago, in my mentoring class, I discovered that the possibility of not being wanted started in the womb. I don't believe rejecting my conception was done intentionally to hurt me. Still, not many women are that thrilled in finding out they are pregnant when their other off springs are teenagers and grown adults. I wondered what was said to me as a fetus or even what words were expressed toward me in the womb. I believe anger was embedded inside of me for a long period of time. My angered responses could be either verbal or non-verbal. Angry because of different experiences and disappointments. Angry because of challenges after challenges always knocking at my door. Angry because I often felt picked on in public. It was awhile before I understood why I was so defensive. I felt I better protect and guard myself from being hurt or ridiculed. I had to protect myself from the wolves. Then it seemed like I would make mistakes trusting people that didn't really love me. I tried to be perfect but often failed. No one really knew how inadequate I always felt because of my ill behavior. I was trying to be perfect so people could stop judging me. Then I was worried about how I looked. Being overweight and my messed-up skin were continual issues. I felt ugly on the inside, and I looked ugly on the outside. I had feelings inside that were confusing and made no sense to me. I have always been hard on myself because others would tell me I needed to be better. I felt pressured from several entities until I stopped listening to opinionated voices. I had to shut a lot of people down. Yes, I made mistake after mistake and said things that often came out wrong. No one knew nor cared how hard I worked at doing things correctly. I didn't mean to hurt anyone. I lashed out because of the pain I had inside. My ill behavior and being rejected ushered me into wanting to crawl into a hole and just disappear forever.

What I learned is not to take people's words or opinions personal. The lesson that I also learned was because I had a broken heart my perception of things could sometimes be off.

My emotions would control my thoughts, causing a whole movie of deception to take place in my brain. Being analytical and introvert is not always the best mix. Truth be told, sometimes, forgiving is easier for some than for others. My desire is to move on, forgiving and releasing all types of anger, disappointment, and every bit of offense that I have experienced. So, whatever I have felt or maybe still somewhat feel, I am intentionally forgiving and releasing people and situations. My responses are destined to be healthy and positive. I will not hold a grudge nor ill feelings against anyone or even against any situation that I have had to encounter. I am not completely there, but I am becoming. Being at peace is my goal. Having joy is so important to me at any cost. I decree and declare that all negative responses and actions in my life are coming to an end. I have begun a new life with and without some people. I have had to face some ugly things that have latched themselves onto a highly creative, beautiful woman. This is my season. I have to dig me out of stuff. And it all started with forgiving.

It took some time for me to work on my patience, endurance, to shut my mouth, forgive and, let go of many things, even letting go of toxic people. Anything that was negative, that took me into a dark place I removed from my life. I have endured much of what many could not see and sometimes what I could not even talk about. I had to learn that if I wanted this cycle to end, there were inner and outer things I had to kill and destroy. I had to step back and pursue the Lord to speak to my mind, speak to my heart, and yes speak to my emotions. I learned I was drowning, I learned from a lot of my physical, mental, and emotional pain. I learned that if I didn't tackle some truths I could die. And it is not my time to die. Many times, having too many emotions and having too many thoughts was bothersome. They both operated on overload. They affected my physical health and even my state of mind. Thoughts and feelings make a person physically and mentally sick. I had to become the captain of my thoughts and my reactions. Why? I was repeatedly feeling rejected. Rejection would not leave. Rejection made me feel like I always had to protect myself. Rejection made me feel unloved. Rejection made me angry and made me feel alone. I often was annoyed that I had the heart to love people who did not love me back. I asked God to allow me to care a lot less. I honestly woke up sad and sometimes annoyed, wanting not to care about others. Why forgive people who hurt others? Why forgive when they didn't apologize? Why forgive someone when they evaluate their lack of remorse of what they have knowingly done to another individual? Yeah, someone may say that's on you if you're hurting. They may say that it isn't their problem if you are hurting. They may even say it's not that big of a deal. Or someone may say just get over it. People may say all sorts of things that could add onto the already painful offense. But what matters is letting go and move on.

Even if you're unsure if someone deserves to be forgiven or not, forgive the person anyway. Forgive yourself. Let go of situations. Even forgive God. Forgive them all because it is a release for you. Forgiveness is not for who you are angry with. Forgiving is release for the individual that was hurt. Forgiving someone is for the person that was victimized. Holding on to forgiveness is a weight and it is a barrier. Holding on to forgiveness clogs a flow from full potential. Lack of forgiveness causes stress. It can cause a headache, a heart attack, more serious diseases, and death. Do you think someone is not worthy of being forgiven? Guess what? They are **not worth** you being stressed out about or losing sleep over either. They probably are getting a good night's sleep and not even thinking about you or what happened to you.

We live in an imperfect world with so many sick minded, selfish people. And many times, hurt people hurt others. If the person refuses to change, pluck them out of your life. Say their name out loud and state that you forgive them and what you forgive them for. It may not be easy. If you believe that you can never forgive someone, then you are holding on to anger or bitterness in your heart. Yes, it can be a process. It may not happen overnight. But try, and try some more. Eventually one day forgiveness will pay the mortgage in your heart. Otherwise, anger and bitterness will fester inside. Holding on to such a dynamic becomes an enemy against you and possibly a strong hold inside of you. The bitterness of not forgiving others can cause sickness and even cause an unwanted disease in your body. So many negative actions and thoughts have roots that grow into ugly branches. Why not become a new tree, bearing wonderful and beautiful fruit? If you refuse to forgive, that is your choice. But you deserve to be free. Why go around captive in your own mind and a prisoner to negative thoughts and negative emotions? Let it go. Don't be stubborn. Let them go. Release it from your heart, from your mind, and from your emotions. You deserve to be happy and, baby, you deserve to live a life full of unspeakable joy. You deserve to be FREE!

One of the reasons I chose to write about my life is that I believe someone needs to hear my story of healing. Someone needs to know that yes, this too shall pass. Someone needs to see that yes, the race is not given necessarily to the swift, not necessarily to the strong. But it is given to the one that has endured. In order for me to heal, one of the major components I have to embrace is forgiving everything. I have made a conscious decision to forgive people, situations, forgive myself, and yes, even forgive God. God!? Why would I need to forgive God? There are times in our lives that yes, we are angry with God. Yes, admit the truth, God already knows how we feel anyway. And admitting the truth always sets us mentally and emotionally free. I needed to acknowledge my anger; otherwise, I would not be able to get past the hurt and to move forward to grow.

CHAPTER 1

And He asked his father, "how long has this been happening to him?" and he said, "from childhood." Mark 9:21

The following is a snapshot of my birth: I was born on Thanksgiving Day to Minnie Ruth Fennell and Levoy Ernest Taylor (The "V" in my dad's name is not a typo). I am also the granddaughter of Eldora Williams Fennell, Rev. Percy Fennell, Mariah Forbes Taylor, and Ernest Levi Taylor. The only one of my grandparents that I ever met was the evangelist Rev. Fennell. That was a setup even then.

The story that is told about that Thanksgiving Day is my mother placed the turkey in the oven, and that is when she went into labor with me. My sisters were preparing to go to the game but could not go since my arrival into the world was much more important. The day of my birth was also on my parents' wedding anniversary. It appeared that I began messing up and changing things from the very beginning. I am the last of the Mohicans as they say.

Children in school teased me, saying I didn't have parents because their parents were younger than mine. This made me angry and secretive about my family. I also was often bullied in school. I was called names and picked on to fight. Negative words were spoken to me: "You weren't meant to be here," "Your dad wanted a boy, not a girl." (What I heard: *your dad didn't want you.*) "You messed up our Thanksgiving when you were born." And "If I was as depressed as you are all the time, I would kill myself." And that is exactly what I tried to do often. I wanted to die, just disappear off of the face of the earth. What was wrong with me that no one loved me? What had I done? Those were the thoughts that weighed heavily on my mind.

During the day, my mom worked, and at night, my dad worked. So, it was my father that walked me to school. And then he walked me home from school at the end of the day. My dad also fixed my lunch and helped me with my homework. He often told me how important having a good education was. So, the importance of education was embedded in me at an early age.

As far back as I can remember, it seemed like I often carried a weight of sadness. Most of the time, I remember being by myself. Most of the time, I had to play by myself. I often felt alone. Loneliness made me angry. Everyone was older than me by a lot of years because I was born late in my parents' lives. My siblings were at least 12 years older and were busy with their own lives. They were always going out, and who wanted a little sister tagging along? It appeared that everyone was too busy for someone as young as me. Stealing my family from me wasn't fair.

Playing alone became a regular pastime. I loved playing with my dishes. I also had a play dining room set and a pretend stove. I would set the table. I would place my dolls at the dinner table and serve them tea. My biggest, favorite doll Tina could walk. She would sit at the head table for tea time. I named my doll after my favorite older cousin whom I adored. I still have my favorite doll today.

I am sure my parents loved me in the best way that they knew how. After all, I was a gift from God. They loved me by feeding and clothing me. I never went around looking neglected nor dirty as if I were not wanted. Not to mention, my parents loved me enough to send me to school to get a good education, and they also taught me about God. There's no greater love that anyone can have than to tell someone about Jesus. I fell in love with God and church. It was my happy place. As a little girl, I was singing gospel songs on the choir. I also learned bible stories about Adam and Eve, Noah, Jesus' birth, his death, and his resurrection. We were in church every Sunday. It was exciting watching and hearing the choirs sing. I loved gospel music. But I loved music period. I believed my interest in music came from my dad.

Truth be told, I do remember fun times with my older sisters. One sister taught me how to tie my shoes and taught me a few songs. Another sister taught me how to spell. She also took me to her Saturday choir rehearsals. My sisters have often rescued me from stuff. They have also been a great support system.

There was a time when my oldest sister took me and my niece to the movies. Even though I messed up the fun by running out of the theater scared of the monster on the screen. This happened only during the commercial. The main movie feature had not yet started. Since I refused to go back inside, we all had to leave. I was a very scary child with a vivid imagination. All things pictured in my mind came to life. Even certain shapes that I saw on the wall looked like faces with leering eyes watching me. It was a curse but yet a blessing at the same time. Now that I am older, I learned that it was an elementary gift of discernment. Not to mention, my imagination became an instrument latched to my artistic creativity.

My oldest sister also took her daughter and me to Atlantic City when we were little. She had been drinking and was rather mouthy to the cops, which almost got us arrested. We were changing our clothes in the public bathroom, which was against the beach's rules.

I believe because my niece and I begged the cops to not take my sister in, they let her go. Plus, she finally silenced her crazy talk.

In Mary Mary's song, "Thank You," the duo sings, "Tragedies are commonplace; all kinds of diseases, people are slipping away." I understood this all too well. In 1988, my oldest sister had a stroke and developed an aneurysm. It was painful watching her in a comatose capacity month after month hooked up to tubes and machines. We watched her deteriorate before our very eyes. On top of all that, plus dealing with an aneurysm, my oldest sister had also contracted pneumonia. After a year of being in the hospital, the Lord took my oldest sister away while my mother sang to her.

Along with three sisters, I had two brothers who lived out of the state from the time I was born, so I really didn't get to know them that well. At the age of 39, my oldest brother passed from a heart attack. I was confused because he wasn't old enough to have a heart attack. When the news was given to me, I couldn't talk. Instead, I went straight to my room. I believe I was in shock. That was my first real experience as an adult losing a close relative to death.

In 2001, I was shocked yet again when I was told that I had another brother. My brother-in-law said he found some guy who had the same name as my dad. And *Levoy* is not a common name. Getting to know my new brother was cool. I finally had a brother in the same city that

I lived in. Plus, he was only five years older than me, so my new brother helped close that age gap with my siblings. Not to mention, he and I had some things in common like our love for music and technology, especially computers. We had my brother in our lives for about six years before we got a call that he had a heart attack and died.

All I could think was now I had three deceased siblings.

CHAPTER 2

From the time I was born, something periodically always appeared to be happening to me. In my adult life, I was told that someone had spoken a curse over my mom when she was pregnant with me. Then years later as an adult, I was told someone put something in my food that was supposed to take me out of here. That might explain strange happenings in my life; I wasn't sure. But for some reason, the news didn't startle me. One of my friends told me once that I was too nonchalant about stuff. Oftentimes, things just rolled off my back.

Pain and life-or-death situations seemed to follow me—sometimes because of my own actions. My first personal experience with death is unknown to me, but I learned that I had contracted a fever of 102 at 2 months old. The doctors had to place me on a bed of ice; the heat coming from my body continually turned the ice into a liquidated state. My family's fear was that I would die—talk about lying on a bed of affliction. But I survived—as you can see.

I was a very inquisitive child who was always doing something with my Curious George self. I was just a busybody. As an infant, I owned a musical lamp that sat by my crib. When the music played, the little girl's arms moved up and down as though she were playing the piano keys. I guess the light bulb fascinated my eyes. It was because of the lamp bulb that today I still have a keloid on my right wrist. This accident occurred by the hot light bulb falling on my wrist while my dad was supposed to be watching me. Mom was at work. (Mothers, never leave your babies with their fathers.) I don't know how the lamp ended up on my wrist. I just know my mother told me she was not happy coming home to find out her baby had been burned. My mother wanted to have the keloid removed, but my pediatrician warned her that there was a chance the scar could return and grow larger. I didn't know, but I had wondered if my dad was in the doghouse for that.

From the top of the stairs at the age of 3, I tumbled down a flight of stairs. My mother froze as she watched me flip over a good amount of twelve steps. When I reached the third bottom step, I jumped down on my own two feet. I guess I figured I better rescue myself. No one else was coming to save me. It was like sister-girl, you're on your own.

Burning my wrist was not the first time experiencing being burned. For whatever reason, I had a strong fascination with chemicals. I was quite the scientist. Hanging out with the bathroom medicine cabinet was one of my dates. I would lock the door and be in there mixing magic in a Dixie cup. I enjoyed watching the reactions of mixing chemicals. This may be why I did so well in all my chemistry classes. Another thing, I was also fascinated with the different pretty colors of fire that paraded from a lit match, then when the match blew out, the dancing, amazing twirling smoke presentation into the air. One night at about 7 years old, while I was supposed to be going to sleep, I got an idea. Guess who snuck out of bed and found her some matches? I wondered how fast I could run from my bedroom to the bathroom with lit toilet paper before the paper burned up. Before ready-set-go, I first filled the bathroom basin up with water. This was the destination for where the lit paper would land. From my room, I did not hesitate to dash down the hall toward the bathroom after setting fire to some toilet paper. Well, unfortunately, this was one of my unsuccessful experiments. Why didn't this smart one know that paper burns fast, especially thin toilet paper? I literally learned when you play with fire you can get burned.

With burnt thumbs, I took my hind parts to bed. I was aching and in so much pain but too afraid to tell my parents about my not-too-smart scientific performance. Since the pain was severe, I could not sleep. I had no choice but to rat on myself. Maybe suffering with burned thumbs kept Mom from lighting more fire to my skin. Instead, she treated my hands with ointment, then placed white socks over my hands before sending me to bed. To this day, I have scars on my thumbs to remind me of my failure to stop, drop, and roll.

In the past, I have snuck out of bed for much more pleasant adventures. Every Monday night, my parents had gospel rehearsal in our living room. My dad along with four other church deacons founded a singing group before I was born called the Gospel 5. I would lay at the top of the steps listening to them accompanied by the pianist from the church. By my teenage years, their wives were singing with them. This would include my own mother. Their rehearsals literally shook our house. I loved listening to their Rock Daniel songs. And the pianist could pick up any song by ear, changing keys to fit someone's voice range, but he had to bang on the floor with his foot to keep his timing. I am sure my parents' singing group was my first musical influence.

By 5 years old, I was performing in front of audiences. First, my mom signed me up for a Tom Thumb wedding. This was some type of fundraiser at our church that triggered my other interests in learning lines for productions. There were two plays that I remembered playing in as a child. In one, I played an angel telling folks that Jesus had risen from the dead. In another production, I played a bad girl that the devil had come to take with him. Talk about someone screaming their head off. I had to fight this adversary back. Sounds like my real life.

My childhood had many twists and turns. I know there were good days. The problem was those were the days I vaguely remembered. It was years before I remembered one summer that my parents allowed me to go down south to spend time with my cousins. We went to the pool almost every day. I remember them teaching me how to swim. I loved the water and loved fishing over on a bridge not far from my aunt's house. I loved my aunt. She was one major reason for wanting to spend my summer down South. Plus, I really grew to love my cousins, too. Unfortunately, it was the same time I experienced being molested by an adult cousin who made me feel very uncomfortable. He was always looking and smiling at me, saying, "You're so pretty." I did not remember this experience until I was an adult. I always wondered why my mom said I kept asking her when was she coming to get me. Now I know exactly why. I desperately wanted to come home.

From this moment on, my life changed. I did not know this cousin's words would lead to him taking me to his home, feeling all the way past my thighs and climbing on top of me. His hot breath was burning my skin as his uncovered bareness poked me and tugged at my panties. I was eight and terrified. Because of his heavy weight pressing down on me, breathing was a challenge. I froze. I remembered not being able to speak. I remember feeling something protruding against my lower body. But someone knocked on the front door, and he jumped off top of me, warning me that I better not tell. Why would I tell? Who would believe me? People didn't listen to children much. We were taught children are to be quiet. The youngest was usually invisible and ignored anyway. Not to mention in many families, secrets are kept quiet and not discussed. Since I blamed myself, I told myself that what he did was my fault. I suspected that others would say I deserved what I got. Didn't I mess up everyone's day by being born? I was always in the way. Unintentional rejection seeped inside me deeper than before.

After becoming an educator and an advocate against bullying, I learned that children/youth (1) need to be heard no matter what and (2) it is neglectful and abusive for anyone to be made to keep that type of violation a secret. No one's reputation is more important than another's personal space or dignity. Our ancestors knew a lot but were unlearned that negative seeds could be planted and manifested. Being in a hostile environment or not protecting a child from the boogeyman creates so much damage in them.

Around 1966, we left our old church to join another church. A few years later, I accepted Jesus Christ as my personal Savior and was baptized when I was about nine years old.

The services at our new church were exciting. I also found it fascinating to hear this one woman speaking in this strange language. I couldn't understand a word she was saying. I thought she was drunk. I remember people used to look at her strange while she seemed in another zone. It made no sense to me that my mom had a drunk friend who was a church member. But I knew I sure liked to see her speaking in this zone. I later learned this woman was not drunk. She was a missionary who spoke in an unknown language from the Holy Ghost. It appeared that the church did not approve of the Holy Ghost showing up in service. Then there was this young man who I used to watch dancing in the spirit. I found watching people dance in the spirit intriguing. Wow, he sure could pick them feet up and put them down. I was amazed at how fast his feet kept up with the beat of the music until he fell into the radiator. I thought he was drunk, too. Every Sunday, he would knock down a bunch of chairs, or he would fall behind the radiator.

Were people really supposed to carry on this way in church? I wasn't sure, but he sure was hilarious to me.

Some of the major things that drew my attention in church was watching the choir directors. I found them fascinating. My sister told me I used to sit on the floor when I was about 3 years old, pretending to direct choirs.

Growing up in our new church gave me a place of belonging. As I got older, I joined the Angelics and Faith Ensemble choirs. Lord, did I love singing on faith. We often got to travel and sing with gospel celebrities. It was just a great singing experience for me.

My group of friends were increasing. Being at our new church brought me many connections that I am still somewhat connected to this day. Back then, I even had a couple of boyfriends. One of my major sweeties was adopted by a couple in our church. I was only twelve. Most of the young people often made fun of his big forehead. But it didn't matter to me since we really liked each other and enjoyed long conversations. Unfortunately, my heart broke when he was sent away. I wasn't able to see nor talk to him anymore. I had no idea where they had shipped him off to. I later found out that he was sent to a group home. I was crushed and sad all over again.

Just like anyone else, I lost and gained friends. I always had lots of people around me, but I have always been very selective with whom I hung out with and called my friend. After so many disappointments with folks, I learned folks will change up on you quick. So, my circle was, and still is, very small. I've learned that I was created to be an awesome friend. I was made to be loyal and integral with a heart to give, but I had to learned only a chosen few were picked to be my real friends. After learning so much, you stop long enough to listen to your inner teacher. You learn to follow a different road. It's essential to learn how to guard your heart. Most of the true friends that I have were handpicked by God for me. And I did not ask for add-ons—and still don't. In 1969, we moved from North Philly to West Oak Lane Philadelphia. Good Lord Jesus, it appeared to be the longest ride on Earth to get from one place to the next. I was not happy about moving from my old house. I didn't understand that where we were moving to was considered upscale from where we had moved from. All I knew was it took me away from what was familiar.

Twenty-First Street was totally the opposite of Reese Street in so many ways. The new street had trees and grass, and the homes sat up much higher above a lawn. On Reese Street, I had 'to scrub steps, but on 21st Street, the steps were concrete. Two things that I did like that were different was our house had a back porch with a driveway, and we also had a garage, which I had never seen before. It was crazy that not only did we live in a house, but also my parents' car also had its own house away from harm, fire, and theft.

What had not changed was I still had to walk to school, but no one walked with me like my dad had done. I hated my new school. I got bullied a lot. Fighting was not my forte, and I avoided fighting like the plague. I did not like the attention or the way fighting made me feel. Then I was bused to another school for a reason I didn't know why. The next school wasn't much better. I was bullied there as well. My memory of sixth grade was being pushed into the corner of the school building during recess. My eye swelled up so bad that it closed completely on its own demand. The only thing I remembered when it happened was seeing stars and having a horrible headache. Plus being guided to the nurse's office. From that day on, I have no other recollection of anything else.

CHAPTER 3

Like the average teenager, I began having unnerving challenges. My moods and hormones were ricocheting around depending on where I was emotionally. I didn't understand the conflicting feelings that were bouncing around inside. I was chubby, and acne was taking over my face. Some creature named Puberty came to live inside my body without my permission. Being bullied in junior high school had escalated. The boys at school teased me and called me names. There were things going on in my life that made no sense. I wasn't quite the social butterfly, nor was I the popular girl that guys wanted to talk to. I was rather shy. But two girls came along that taught me new things like how to smoke cigarettes.

On the way to and from school, my new friends were trying to teach me how to blow smoke out of my mouth without swallowing. A few times, we drank Johnny Walker on the way to school. I remember being sick as a dog when I got to school, and I had to lay on the floor. I was tore up. Smoking cigarettes became common. I could smoke like a pro. I had become someone else that even I didn't recognize.

I hated life, and it was as if no one saw the heaviness I felt. I could not shake this hurt off. Every day, I began cutting myself with a razor. I no longer could tolerate these inside triggers that made me feel abnormal. I even felt embarrassed about my sexual curiosity. I would just sit in the bathroom crying, watching my blood rise through my pores. The next day, I started cutting my hand all over again. I didn't want to live, but I was too afraid to die and go to hell. Thank God, one of the NTAs at school took interest in me and took me under her wing. NTAs were there to assist with disciplining students. I'm not sure why she ever went beyond her duties when helping me. Maybe she saw something in me. This woman was rather loving and became my confidant. I felt like I could trust her without being judged. I knew nothing about puberty. At least if I had heard about it, I did not know who she was. But Puberty was a stranger to me that made my life a living hell. I did not like Puberty, and she was a cruel heifer.

My mom must have known I was acting odd. I had become rather rebellious, smoking and talking back. I remembered one of the church leaders threatening to slap me, and my mom told this woman that she better not put a hand on her child. If there was a problem with me, my mom said she would handle it. But my mother must have gotten tired of trying to handle me. Obviously, I was depressed, crazy, and disrespectful. So, Mom released me to my dad for him to handle my behavior. I ended up being sent to a child therapist. I don't remember what went on with my treatment there. I'm not even sure if the sessions were successful. I just remember being sick of life.

My dad spent a lot of time talking and grooming me. Instead of spanking me, he'd talk to me for hours. I'd sometimes rather he had spanked me than having those conference meetings with him. Mom believed in lighting fire to my behind. But my dad was more prone to lectures. His lectures were torture, which to me was punishment. I remember once saying to my dad he should record a movie, *"Why I Talk So Much."* Everyone bust out laughing thinking my comment was hilarious. This time, however, Dad did not crack a smile. My mouth had gotten me in trouble numerous times. Sometimes, it still does. Later in life, I had to teach myself to think first before letting venom come out of my mouth.

As a teenager, I fooled around with boys a little too early for my britches. My boyfriend who lived across the driveway from us moved to New Jersey, and I didn't remember him telling me that he was moving. He sent me a letter saying that he still loved me and would come back to visit. Lies and deception. He did come back, but by that time, he was married to some girl, and they had two kids. He told me that he did not love his wife. He said that the only reason he had married her in the first place was because she got pregnant, and the second child was an accident. I didn't believe him. It didn't matter why he got married. What mattered to me was that he could no longer marry me. He was stolen from me. I was angry that he left and allowed it to happen. I could not understand why people kept leaving me. How do you guard your heart from being destroyed? If ya not gonna stay, why bother at all? I often questioned God about why he allowed people in my life who would hurt me. I didn't adapt to hurt too well, and I suffered in silence. As much as I didn't talk about my pain, I believed everyone should have a person whom they can share their feelings with. In times past, I had expressed these feelings in unhealthy ways. One of my favorite guys to mess around with lived a couple of blocks away. I didn't see him as often as I liked. Nor did I see him enough to say he was my boyfriend. When he called, I made myself available. I just snuck out the house when my parents were asleep. My mother didn't like him. She said he looked too old for me because he had a full beard. Actually, he was only four years older than me. Mom didn't stop me from seeing this 19-year-old when we wanted to see each other. He had a car, and he would come pick me up. I only saw him at night, usually after 11 p.m. We hung out at different spots, including his apartment. What were we doing?

Momma would not have been happy, and my father probably would have killed us both. My dad almost found him hiding in our basement once. I just knew my friend and I were gonna die that day. But my sexual maintenance man got out of the house in the nick of time. To me, that was love. He was a male peer who was taking time to be with me. And he patiently took the time to show me that he loved and that he cared for me.

I learned many years later that my male friend ended up in rehab, struggling with a drug addiction. The last time I saw him he had lost a lot of his teeth. I guess he couldn't afford to buy any. 'No teeth' is not sexy. The man could not afford a car, so he got around on a bike. He had lost his apartment and had to move back home with his momma. The last time I remember seeing him he said to me, "Lynn, you look good." And he was absolutely right. I looked marvelous. God has been gracious to me. Before any more spoken words, I got away from dude quickly. I fled. Whether he had teeth or not, the way he called my name still made me melt. Run, Forrest!

CHAPTER 4

I didn't play outdoors like other children. A lot of my physical activity was going to the skating rink with the young people in my church or going to the bowling alley with the kids in the neighborhood. Most of my activities, however, were in my room doing one of my three favorite things: reading, writing, or listening to music.

To this day, I love reading; I have my very own home library with about 300 books. My fifth-grade teacher recognized how much I loved books. She wrote on my report card once, "Lynda loves to read; buy her a lot of books." I remember my first genre of interest was Sci/Fi. But that changed because the romance/love bug must've bit me.

The birth of my desire to write came from being sent to my room on punishment. I remember one of my first written stories was about talking shoes, which I earned an "A." So sending myself to my room became wonderful. Writing also became a portion of my survival kit. I was a troubled soul, so I made up my own pretend world that consisted of true, dependable, safe love. I first began writing poems. I called myself writing stories, but they were written in play form. I was unaware that literary writings had different formats. I began learning how to write in third, first, and second person. I was writing long novels. I even journaled in the difficult times of my life. Writing, I found, was very therapeutic for me. Seriously, I can't live in peace without not being able to write for any long period of time. Writing appears to be an obsession for me. I was told by a friend that my writing is my passion, which made sense because I do love to write.

Writing all the time as I did got me into trouble sometimes. I was writing during choir rehearsal not paying attention to the songs being taught. Or I could be in math class writing a story or a play instead of doing my math classwork. My attention would be compromised of creating a story or a play. I would be writing any and every place. I would get ideas from sermons. Many of my stories have come from my dreams. I could have a dream, wake up, and create a whole story out of it. I would find it intriguing how my imagination birthed such creativity forming from a world of fantasy.

Then I would also be found blasting music in my room. My dad, his singing group, my piano teacher, and my first gospel choir director from junior high school obviously were my first teachers and influences in regard to music. They all left such an impact on me that led to my deep interest in music, directing choirs, and playing the piano. I also had interests in sound equipment. My dad owned microphones and a reel to reel tape recorder. So, when I turned about 10, I also owned my first reel to reel tape recorder and a Polaroid camera.

I ate music all day. It was a portion of my survival kit. My parents sang. My sister and my brother also sang. I had other relatives that sang. And I also sang on church, school, and community choirs. I was on four choirs all at once in my 20s. Yet, I was also suicidal, and nobody knew it. The perfect outlet for me at 12 years old was the junior high school's gospel choir. I was excited about joining. The woman leading the choir not only was an evangelist, but she also had a love for young people. Singing with my junior high school gospel choir was a pivotal time in my life. Learning voice techniques began to turn my life around. Being on this type of choir made a positive impression on me. It was the only thing that made going to school worthwhile because the daily bullying I received sure wasn't one bit enjoyable. I had been in the midst of Baptist folk all my life. But the experience of being around Pentecostal folk was different. My junior high school choir director was Pentecostal. They danced in the Holy Ghost and spoke in a heavenly language led by the Holy Ghost. All of this intrigued me. People didn't talk much about the Holy Ghost in my church, but I was interested in knowing more about the power that geared people to dance and speak in an unknown tongue from God. My membership on the choir was changing my life in many ways. I wasn't self-inflicting myself with a razor as much. I began to have a true reason to live.

My genuine love for music continued to grow, promoting a strong drive of wanting to bang on those black and white piano keys. I loved the sound that the piano made. I begged my mother enough that she finally allowed me to take piano lessons. My first teacher was some professor that I did not like. He was a horrible teacher who scratched me. I had no idea why he scratched me. Maybe it was an accident, but he sure didn't apologize. My most memorable teacher was a little lady whose fingers danced across those black and white keys. She was one of the most elegant women I had met. I never understood how those short little fingers created such powerful music. My fingers were longer than hers, and I could not bang on those keys the way she could. She had a lot of spunk, but she was also rather strict. My private lessons took place in her home. I used to love coming to her gorgeous house. She had such poise and style. Her home reminded me of a museum. She obviously admired antiques. I knew if I practiced and did what she taught me I would become an awesome pianist. But I couldn't get the hang of certain things. Keeping the timing and figuring out the beats for certain musical notes was challenging and discouraging. I was annoyed that I could not play by ear. I knew music in my head, but I didn't seem to be able to articulate it on the keys. It just wasn't fair that some people could listen to a song a few times then pick up chords and begin playing. Those folks got on my nerves, ha! Lord, I felt cheated. Even though I did not have that ability, there was no doubt components of music had been embedded inside of me. As the scripture states, your gift will make room for you. Believe me, my gifts were presenting themselves in a powerful way.

As a young child, I directed to songs on tapes in my room over and over. I heard music playing in my dreams. This led me to becoming the youngest paid choir director in our church. I was even assigned to directing the adult choirs in our church as a teenager. My sister told me how people watched and were memorized when I directed. That took me by surprise. I was only doing what I believed God led me to do. I was told I directed with my whole body.

The church I grew up in had an annual program called the Night to Remember, which was a concert where all the choirs in the church sang. The Night to Remember became so in demand that we had to have an afternoon and evening program. During that time, there were 11 choirs in our church, which yours truly was assigned to direct most of them. So, because I directed hard with my whole body, most of the time, I was very, very sore the next day. I felt like someone who had spent a whole day in the gym doing aerobics. Aerobics for Jesus!

Some of my directing assignments caused several of the male directors to disapprove of my being a part of the music department and made trouble for me. Another young lady was also involved, but no one really approved of her involvement either, including the young people. But the kids loved me. I learned that I didn't have to always fight my own battles. All I had to do was keep using my abilities and be integral to my life and the lives of others

During this period of my life, I identified that I had valuable skills. Writing, singing on the choir, and directing were very therapeutic. My skills made me feel acceptable in the world. I was learning that I was very creative. Writing became a passion for me.

Everyone should dig inside to find what talent or gift that brings them joy and peace. It is vital. Dig for how to fill the empty spot that is felt inside. Every individual has the need to be empowered and to grow. We all have goodness inside that can help ourselves and others. Plus, these talents that we have were placed there to give us opportunities to release tension that lingers in the mind, in the emotions, and in the heart. Not having a safe way to effectively blow off steam can be unhealthy physically, mentally, or emotionally.

CHAPTER 5

High school was a propelling ride for me. I did well in my academics, graduating with my diploma and also receiving a certification from a two-year work-study program while in high school; the governmental program taught distribution of merchandise, and it gave high school students an opportunity to take classes on distribution, math, and English in the morning; have lunch; and then work in a huge clerical office.

Outside of my high school classes, the students had a blast. For me, basketball games, my friends, drama, and choir were the best of my world. I would say those three years were the most exhilarating times of my life. My old boyfriend from church had somehow popped up while I was in junior high school, just reappearing just like he had disappeared. But we weren't interested in each other anymore. Did I still like him and boys? Absolutely, but they basically were on the back burner of my life then. My days were filled with a crew of fun friends and other activities. I was a teenager; social time was the most pivotal time of my life! No time for a boyfriend.

One of my favorite activities in high school was being in the drama club learning theater. Our performances were performed in the high school auditorium. In one play, this girl was acting and laughing so hard that, in front of an audience, she went to sit, and her chair folded up on her. Down she went hard on the floor. Everyone lost their composure. I was no more good after that.

High school was different than junior high school. I was so glad I had graduated from there. I thought I would kill myself if I got left back. I hated junior high school. It was a horrific time in my life. High School Gospel Choir was different; for one, there was no adult in charge like we had in junior high school. The young man in charge, however, was a good friend of mine. It was obvious that my friend was seriously on fire for the Lord. We didn't just sing during choir rehearsal. Young people were accepting Christ as their personal savior and tarrying for the Holy Ghost. One afternoon while tarrying, worshipping, and praising God, I will never forget seeing this bright light that obviously only I saw. I was about 16 years old. The light was all around me as if I were inside of it. It was during this particular rehearsal/service when for the first time I experienced speaking in an unknown tongue. Similar to what that lady did in our old church so long ago when I was a little girl. I never talked about that experience to anyone being no one would probably believe me. My parents never talked about speaking in tongue nor the Holy Ghost. I did share the experience with my pastor's wife years later. I was sitting in her office, and she had asked me had I ever had a special encounter with God. When I shared with her about seeing a light and speaking in tongue, her eyes grew the size of flying saucers. Obviously, she was intrigued.

I went to my prom with my old boyfriend that had disappeared from church then popped up in junior high school. We had a blast. My parents gave me one of the best graduation presents. Several of us from the church ended up on a plane to California, which included going to Hollywood, Disneyland, and Universal Studios.

Being in Hollywood was cool. My favorite place on the trip was Universal Studios. It was an awesome place for a person with a large imagination like me to spend a day. Inside the campus were actual movie and TV shows where actors and actresses made things happen. We saw where the movie *Jaws* was made, *The Taking of Pelham 123*, and *The Ten Commandments*. How awesome to see the way they divided the Red Sea. And to have Jaws jump out of the water while in a fake, sinking tour boat. We also were shown TV tricks that are sometimes used while taping. While in Hollywood, they showed us so much make-believe stuff, watching TV was ruined for me.

So, by the time I came back to Philly, I had lost interest in watching television for several weeks.

There will be times in our lives when we will have unforgettable, teachable, happy nuggets to glean from. They can come in a package of milestones and great accomplishments. For some, they may even come in the midst of chaos. Those are nuggets to keep hidden in your heart for when you have uncertainties about yourself, uncertainties about others, and uncertainties about relationships, among other things. Just know that everyone's uncertainties will be different. I guarantee the uncertainty will come. But learn not to allow them to throw you permanently under the bus.

CHAPTER 6

When I turned 18, I thought I was grown. There was some type of shift that took place again within me. I had decided that I had enough of school and would put off going to college for the time being. The friends I was mostly with at that time were folks I worked with, sang with, and got high with. I'm not even sure who introduced me to marijuana. But I bought a nickel bag or a dime bag every day or every other day. I wasn't much of a drinker. I didn't like how too much liquor intake caused a person to act. But getting high to me was a horse of another color. I enjoyed the feeling of being on cloud 9. I wasn't high all the time, but I would get high just about every day.

I learned how to roll a joint, and I would do that or smoke reefer out of a pipe. All I had to do was put a little reefer in the top, light it, and inhale. Even though I never smoked cigarettes around my parents, I guessed they knew about my cigarettes. I doubt, however, they knew I was getting high. My dad did question once about this strange smell in my room. I had the window wide open. I made up some cock and bull story that the smell was coming in from outside. Dad didn't question me. But I don't know whether he believed me or not.

Instead of going to college, a close friend of mine got me a job with her at Gino's. Mom loved me working there since I would be allowed to bring home a huge bag of chicken. She loved Gino's chicken. I enjoyed working there because it was a fun place to work. Most of us got along and laughed often. I learned how to use most of the appliances including the slicer for the roast beef sandwiches. We were also responsible for cleaning the equipment at night and taking the appliances apart. I knew how to do these steps well. Yet one evening my middle finger slipped on the blade I was cleaning. Oh my God, I had not bled like that since I had a nose bleed when I was a little girl. At a certain age, I was prone to long nose bleeds that would not stop. During that time, I was diagnosed as anemic. Well, when I cut my finger wide open, the blood would not stop. Nothing we did was successful. Once the paramedics came, I had no choice but to give them the bird since I had injured my middle finger. Maybe I was being punished for using the bird too much. The bleeding finally was stopped. I was given paper stitches and wrapped with gauze bandages.

Another job I got that was rather comical was one making trophies. It was a bit intriguing to use those different types of machinery that made several shapes to the metal for certain trophies. I couldn't get the hang of that job. Speed was very important, and keeping my fingers was more important to me. Once I quit, I never looked back, not once.

Getting high was not my only enjoyment at that time. Traveling and singing with a huge choir was a blessing and an awesome experience. Our choir was often chosen to sing with various professional recording artists, and we also sang once for a production at the Merriam Theater in downtown Philly.

I finally made it to being a grown up. That was true. I had finally grown up to the level where I could make my own decisions without being questioned. I didn't have to report to anyone. There were adults that had suggested I go to school. But I didn't want to be told what to do anymore, so I chose not to go to college. Any opportunity that allowed me rebel in life, I took. I do not like rules and regulations. I didn't want to be chained to books. I was finally free. I had been kept in a cage for so long. This bird enjoyed being free and doing whatever I wanted. And I went wherever I wanted to go without having to check in with my parents on where I was going. I loved it! "Girls just wanna have fun." And I was that girl.

But procrastination can create chaos. I was having fun—that was true. However, some of that fun didn't really get me anywhere. I was wasting valuable time.

There are some fun choices that we make that can cause a delay. I ended up so off course from not going to college. I still regret that.

CHAPTER 7

It took me three years to decide to go to college. One of my close friend's mother, who I called my aunt, kept encouraging me to go back. I spent many hours in her home with her three daughters, the two oldest being my closest friends. Auntie was a nurse, wife, mother, and a first lady. She was a good listener. I was very frank with her. But I never shared with her about my getting high journeys. I'm not sure if her daughters even knew about my reefer involvement. I am sure none of them would have approved.

My first classes in college were English, math, and chemistry. I later took on more English classes and added piano courses. Every few years, I was entering some type of course. I decided to stop going to college when my mom had a heart attack. It was taking too long to graduate. What I wanted to do was make a lot of money to help take care of my mother. So instead of staying in college, I was led to enroll in a nursing program for geriatric care. This gave me my medical background. Through that program, I learned how to care for the elderly. We had to learn every bone and muscle, how to give first aid, how to shave a client, how to give needles, take blood, make hospital beds, and the list went on.

I was amazed with how just about the whole class gravitated toward me. Every day during lunch time, a few of us paraded to the nearby park on Walnut Street to share a few puffs of recreational pleasure. Yes, we would be sitting in class high, laughing and giggling but not missing a beat. I kept doing well in all my academics and passed every test. We each coached one another through any challenge. Back then, I did not realize folks thought I had a healthy sense of humor. We became like family. . During this time, I had experienced a huge disagreement with a close friend. That became a huge distraction that kept me from being able to concentrate on my studies. But because we were like family, including our instructor, they guided me through my school work. At graduation, I was blown away with receiving two awards. Guess who was awarded the most popular student and was on the Dean's List? Me.

To complete our nursing program, we all were required to endure two weeks of training in a nursing home. Those two weeks seemed longer than the six-month program. Each nursing home that we trained in was chosen by the head of the nursing program and our instructor. All the popular students were split up. I was sent to a nursing home in the Northeast section of Philadelphia, a place where I did not expect I would survive from the smell. On-the-job training was one thing, but now I had to be in a nursing home, a place where all the patients were not just sick, but also, they were old and sick. I had to be sure this field was for me. Yes, I did well in class. I did great on all my tests. But now working with real clients was a real test. Would I pass?

Ten days dragged like ten years in my mind, but at the end, I became a certified home health aide. Not to mention I would never have to return there. Instead, my girlfriend's husband helped me received employment at a nursing home in Dresher, PA. My parents had given me their old Plymouth Duster so I could drive to work every day. I despised working the 3-11 p.m. shift because it was smack in the middle of the day.

Every day, I wore some type of nursing gear. Back then, there were no printed uniforms; we basically wore white with comfortable white nursing shoes. My duties included everything: making beds, giving baths, assisting with lifting patients and giving showers, using a Hoyer lift for heavy patients, supervising with grooming, feeding clients, caring for bedsores, giving enemas, and anything else that dealt with the livelihood of any resident there that particular day. One thing I was not allowed to do was administer medicine.

There were a few connections that I made in the nursing home on three different levels. I became connected with one of my supervisors, two of my coworkers, and some of the clients. I surprised myself with the fact that I did not mind caring for the elderly. There were some that were bedridden and others in wheelchairs. Sometimes, it was sad watching these older citizens deteriorating. Truth be told and sad to see, but the most of them were Caucasians that seemed not to have families that cared. Most of the time, they didn't have visitors. I didn't usually work on Sundays, but when I did, I hated missing church. I had one client with Parkinson's that could walk but took the slowest baby steps anyone could image. She could speak but not loud enough for anyone to hear her. It took a lot of patience to care for her, but she was a sweetheart. Then there was a client named Dorothy who was a walker that continually tried to escape. We had to watch her like a hawk, especially when she went outside for a smoke. Sarah was a diabetic that had lost both of her legs. It was amazing to watch this little elderly lady maneuver herself from her chair to her bed. She had amazing upper body strength. She was more independent than lots of individuals who owned legs. Violet, now she was feisty. She was the first person I had ever seen dying. Because she was Caucasian, I experienced seeing her turn into a pale ghost, which freaked me out. I was no better for the rest of the evening. There were a few of us who did all we could to save her life, including performing CPR. Pure Violet. There was an old woman there that kept her legs tightly closed all the time. When someone came to care for her, she would always say, "You ain't getting none." I think they said she had been molested or raped.

Then we had a client that used to call all African-American women "girlie." That irked all of us because she appeared to be treating us as if we were working on the plantation. Most of the staff did their best to avoid her because everyone knew how nasty and mean she could be. For some reason, she was not mean to me— I guess because I was always kind to her, and I also helped her with her showers. She was very particular and wanted things done exactly as she asked. Annoying yes, but whatever. Her kindness wore off suddenly one day. Even now, I have no idea what really happened. After one particular weekend, I came back to work, and I had no job. Back then, I used to cuss. "That blankety blank so and so woman" told the supervisor that I did not help her with her shower. I was the only one who *would* help her with her showers. For whatever reason, the woman lied, costing me my job.

Losing that job sent me back to school. This time, I enrolled into a computer school to become a computer operator. Learning how to write computer programs was what the program was really about. I came home with a headache every day. I was not failing, but the classes were extremely hard. Each class was all about using and writing out the correct formulas to command the computer to execute specific actions.

The key was if we did not used the correct computer command then the wrong result would be executed. There were four different computer programs that we learned. One I just could not get right to save my life.

By 1985, I had several different jobs under my belt and had been enrolled in college and had enrolled in two trade schools. I had moved out of my parents' house to live with a close friend and her family because they were closer to my job. I was working at Burger King during that time until after midnight, and then I would get up at six in the morning for my eight o'clock computer class. I never understood how I was capable to continue with such a schedule.

Church and directing the choir was still very much a priority to me. I still had not given up smoking reefer. Shame on me for getting high in between services with a couple of my buddies, but nothing stopped me from directing my young people. Not even smoking a joint. I loved my youth. Sometimes, I would pile them up in my car, and we would church hop. We loved going to services, but my young friends looked up to me, so I kept my Mary Jane smoking a secret.

Going back to school was greatly beneficial for me in so many ways. There is a saying: *What is for you...is for you*, meaning it may be delayed, but not too often will your blessing be blocked. The support I received education-wise from that nursing program I will never forget. When I received such recognition for my hard work from the Dean and staff, it was nothing short of amazing. Out of fifty plus students, I was chosen. To me, that showed confirmation that I was valuable. I was accepted.

Not only that, my accomplishments were empowering me to move forward and helped to broaden my professional horizons.

Now that I was twenty-four years old, it was time for me to be on my own.

CHAPTER 8

My old married ex-boyfriend who had moved to New Jersey did come back in my life. And oh my God, looking at him still melted me inside. I was as crazy about him as I had always been when we were teenagers. This would be the first time I had ever been in a relationship with a married man. My logic was I wanted him, he wanted me, and I had him first. He reminded me that he didn't love his wife and why he married her. Plus, he promised me that he wasn't going back to her, they were getting a divorce, and that he wasn't happy. And I believed him.

This relationship was really no good for me. I was already dealing with depression and mood swings. Him dumping me to go back to his wife after swearing he'd never go back to her didn't help me one bit. Had it not been for God and my sister, I think I would be dead today because I no longer wanted to live. I was on the verge of killing myself.

My married ex-boyfriend had really broken my heart this time. No matter that he apologized several times for lying to me and sat crying along with me. I was still devastated and hurt that he broke up with me. I don't recall ever hurting that bad in my chest before. The anxiety attack I had was overwhelming. I hurt more that second time he left me than the first time when he had moved to New Jersey. But it was really my fault. I should had never been in an intimate relationship with a married man in the first place. I wasn't taught that type of behavior. Another reason I think him dumping me hit so hard was all my girlfriends had boyfriends, and I had no one. I could never understand why I was always alone no matter what. Rejected once again.

My girlfriends seemed to always have success with their boyfriends but not me. If a guy wanted me, it was for sex. But I was slow to indulge—mostly because I feared getting pregnant. My parents promised me if I had a baby out of wedlock I would have to move out. The best way for me to deal with emotional pain was to find and be involved in other outlets. Getting high had become my portion. I realized I needed to focus more on school and getting a job. I was still going to computer school. I also kept my night job cleaning offices. I no longer had my Plymouth Duster because it caught on fire. We believed our next-door neighbor set it on fire being he was always complaining about parking spaces. We had no proof he was responsible for it, but during that time, I was having some problems with my car, and he complained my car was taking up parking.

To get to my night job in Ft. Washington, my mother loaned me her Toyota. I had to drive through the Industrial Park, an area where businesses took over several blocks. My job was located in this area. I was rushing to work, but what happened next had nothing to do with my speed. As usual, I was listening to gospel music. I remember clapping and praising God, having a good time in the Lord on the way to work. I have very little recollection of what happened when I drove around a curve. I do remember repeating "Oh, my mother's car" over and over. I had just been in a head-on collision. But that was not all. The impact from being hit from the front head-on shoved me into another car that was on the side of me. I was sandwiched in, laying on the car seat, crying because I was concerned only about damage to my mother's Toyota. The other thing I was concerned about was missing work.

People were telling me not to move, to just lay still. I was 24 and crying like a newborn baby just spanked on the bottom. Why were things always happening to me? Was I being punished for imperfections in my life? This wasn't even my first car accident. The last accident, some car ran into the back of me as I waited on the ramp to merge onto the expressway. Everyone with good sense knew to wait for traffic to clear before launching out. A few years back, I got pinned on the foot in between two cars. Now, here I was, minding my own business on the way to work, and this young thing jumped her lane and rammed her car head-on into my momma's car. This appeared to be more than just being labeled accident prone.

Once the ambulance arrived, I was scared that I'd be paralyzed. A neck brace was placed on me before I was lifted on a board to be placed into the ambulance. My parents met us at the hospital. I was still on my back, worried about the damage to my mom's car. "We can get another car, but we can't get another you," she had said. True. That sounded nice. But I believed Mom was still pissed that her car had been totaled. It wasn't my fault, but I sure felt responsible. For days, I was sore. But the miracle was as bad as the car looked, I was not hurt; not a visible scratch was on me. All these car accidents needed to stop trying to claim my life. I was alive and terribly in a lot of pain. Too much pain ushered me into quitting school and not working. I also couldn't direct the choir, and I had to wear a stupid neck brace that I hated. At least it wasn't one of those hard neck braces like I had to wear in the first car accident I was in a few years ago. I realized I had been saved from another car accident. No doubt I must have had angels assigned to me.

Physical therapy was three times a week. I began seeing a chiropractor that kept giving me moist heating pad treatments and cracking my neck and my back. Each time I had to lay on a special table during these treatments. My tests from the hospital consisted of X-rays, MRI, and a CAT scan. I even had acupuncture done where pins were stuck in my head. How crazy does that sound? It sounds and maybe looks like pure torture. But I kid you not, I didn't feel a thing.

I wanted to be grown so bad, but being grown appeared to have just as many nightmares as before. I couldn't figure out why I could be enjoying life finally. Then at the blink of an eye, my happiness was stolen from me again!

CHAPTER 9

About a week later after my accident, I received an unexpected phone call. I didn't recognize the voice. It was my supervisor from my night job. He said he was calling because he heard about the car accident. He wondered where I had disappeared to since I had not returned to work. I thought it was rather thoughtful for him to inquire about my incident. One of my coworkers had told me that the supervisor had the eye on me, but I didn't believe him. I mean yeah, this guy called to check on me, but he did not appear to be interested in me romantically in person. I very seldom ever saw him. Wasn't he married anyway, I thought. I had enough of messing around with married men. Once during a conversation between me and my supervisor, I asked why he was walking around not wearing his wedding ring. He told me because he wasn't married. Oh. But he was living with his girlfriend. Oh. I later found out that they weren't getting along very well, plus his mother and family didn't like her. Oh really?

This man was tall, very handsome, and had some of the largest biceps ever. He must have been eating a lot of spinach. We began having other conversations here and there. Our conversations sometimes covered family, work, ambitions, and God. Maybe we were beginning to flirt with each other a little. I knew this guy had a live-in girlfriend, but with the way he said they were arguing, I wondered why they were staying together. Eventually, I asked him just that, inquiring why was he settling for less. He had no comment. Obviously, he wanted things to work out with him and Missy Girl. So, I left further personal conversations with him alone.

A few days later while over my sister's, I received another call from him asking if I wanted to go to the movies. I could have fainted.

"What about your girlfriend, sir?" I asked. He moved out of their apartment and was now staying with his mother. When the girlfriend threw all his clothes out the window, 'the camel's back' had been broken. It made him think about my question. Why was he settling for less? One thing I had to let this guy know was that any man I went out with had to be in church, and he had to love God.

From our first date to the movies, our relationship grew quickly. My new boyfriend came to see me every night after his second job. He even came in the snow. When it was time for me to meet his mom, I was too scared to get out of the car. His mom came running out of the house to greet me. She was so nice and one of the sweetest people' in the world. She definitely became my second mom. In front of him, she told me if he ever acted up to let her know, and she would take care of him.

My boyfriend and I dated for a short period of time. We did things entirely too fast. Looking back, I believe our relationship grew too quickly. I was flabbergasted when he talked to my dad about wanting to marry me. My parents gave their blessing. We had only been together for about six months before getting engaged. We didn't even have marriage counseling, and no one insisted we should go.

It was truly a blessing that we belonged to God. Weddings are expensive and can be rather costly. So many came through for us with either free or discounted deals. We had a limo that my parents did not have to pay for being they were friends of the family. Most of those who sang in our wedding did not charge us. My gown was made by my best friend's mother who paid for my material and everything the dress and I needed. We got a good deal on the reception hall, our invitations, and even the caterer was a friend of the family.

On October 4, 1986, at 4 p.m., I became a married woman. I was an hour late because my bridesmaids were slow. People thought it was my fault, but I was the only one dressed. People called our wedding a Dynasty Wedding. We had 16 people in our wedding party. I was extremely nervous coming down the aisle. I couldn't even look at my future husband as comfortable as I had become with him. My eyes were fixed on the huge wooded, lit cross on the wall. When I walked past, my godmother whispered that I had better not cry. Believe you me, I sucked those tears right back up in my eyeballs.

Our theme song was "Wait for Love." I chose that song because I felt that waiting for love was exactly what I had done even though I was only twenty-five, and since my husband was thirty-six, he also had waited. Not to mention I was crazy about Luther Vandross. Our honeymoon was in the Pocono's. There was so much to do inside and outside the cabin. And we were trying to do it all.

After the honeymoon, I had so many decisions to make and errands to run. I needed to get all my IDs changed over to my new married name. Most important to me, I immediately joined the church where my husband had become a member on Palm Sunday. I didn't want to serve the Lord in a different church than where my husband was. The hardest decision that I had to make was giving up directing my church choirs. It was time to move on. To me, it felt like I was leaving everything to gain nothing.

My youth were upset with me. They didn't understand. Why, just because I had gotten married, did I have to stop being their choir director? I couldn't explain it any more than I already had. It was just what I believed was the right thing I had to do.

Joining my husband's church was the right decision for me to make, but I wasn't happy. I didn't know anyone at this church, and I was so uncomfortable. The singing wasn't even what I was used to hearing. I was used to hearing voices that could sing and carry a note. In other words, it felt painful being there. But out of obedience, I knew it was where I belonged in spite of the overwhelming separation that took place.

On top of dealing with isolation and other emotions, I couldn't figure out why I was feeling so sick. I was spending time trying to figure out who gave me this virus, but those thoughts died the minute my gynecologist confirmed some surprising news: I was pregnant. What!? 'Getting pregnant stopped me from smoking cigarettes and reefer. I was not about to jeopardize the life of my child. I prayed to the Lord to take away the taste and the desire. And God did what I asked. Cold turkey, I stopped. I couldn't stand the smell of cigarettes. It was over. My husband and I were only married a month, and here I was— pregnant. Who does that? This would explain the dizziness and nausea I had been experiencing. We were ecstatic. We definitely didn't plan on starting our family this soon, but it can definitely happen when one tapped into the cooking jar.

I wasn't working on a permanent job at the time. Instead, I was working on temporary job assignments downtown through temp agencies. This made me catch a bus, go down steps to get on the subway, then climb back up steps above the ground, and walk a couple of blocks to the job. This might had been good exercise for a pregnant woman, but it wore me out. I would get tired and nauseous, but I kept pushing my way through the day. I took my prenatal vitamins daily, but I wasn't 'sure if those things really worked. My husband kept working two jobs, so we both were busy developing our finances. We also had our own apartment.

I usually got home about six every day. My husband got home much later than I did, and I hated that, but dinner was always ready for him when he arrived. One thing about me, as much as I wanted my husband home with me, I did know how to occupy my time until he came home.

Being pregnant was a different kind of experience. It wasn't that much fun feeling sick. Still my gyn doctor always gave me a good report that the baby and I were doing well, and I was hopeful.

CHAPTER 10

Being promiscuous will catch up with you one way or the other, trust me. And usually when it catches you, the hayride was not worth the basket of fun. To this day, I cannot explain when this attack on my body festered. I'm not even sure who I lost my virginity to. There were a few significant things in my past that I had forgotten, and I wasn't sure why. On my first prenatal exam, my gyn doctor informed me that I had contracted a virus that would be fatal to my baby's delivery, so for the safety of my child, I would be scheduled for a C-section. That meant cutting me open and subjecting me to major surgery. I had never had major surgery before in my life. So, for months, I was terrified of the what-ifs. Believe me, I prayed that the condition would not hurt my baby and for this monster to go away. I didn't care about the doctor telling me that there was no cure.

Five months pregnant, I was still going up and down the steps to get on the subway. My doctor had said I could continue working. There were lots of women who worked every day while having a baby. Yes, we were all excited about the baby's arrival drawing closer.

It was spring time and not too hot, thank the Lord. I hadn't missed any of my prenatal appointments.

Maybe because I had not been pregnant before, I did not know if something abnormal was going on. I just thought the feelings I was having were part of the pregnancy journey. When the feelings went away, I was relieved. Until that evening in bed when the pain awakened me, and they were brutal. The trip to the bathroom wasn't even the norm. I felt this bubble hanging from me, and I was scared to death. Something was protruding outside of my body. When my husband saw what I saw, we both knew we had to get to the hospital.

The events of that day I was able to express better when given a writing assignment to do in a 45-minute writing class in October 2006. We were given prompts to choose from to create a short story. This was the prompt I chose:

The Suitcase in the Attic

The old suitcase that I found October 14, 2006, in the attic brought back memories that I had abandoned so long ago. This place was cold and quiet. Time had turned to ice. I sat down on the dingy hardwood floor. My palms were clammy and sweaty. Perspiration oozed out of my pores. I could feel my pulse beating in my throat as I unzipped the luggage from my past. The suitcase was designed by Baby Phat and dipped in the color burgundy. I was hesitating about opening the lid, fear of which emotion would gush out.

My old suitcase was full of clothes that were gifts to me at my baby shower. Everyone knew we were having a boy because my husband had insisted on asking my doctor the verdict. I was against unfolding such knowledge because being told the baby's gender would ruin the surprise while the child was forming in my womb. The most important thing to me, more than anything, was that our baby was healthy.

I remember the day when the doctor announced that my blood test was positive. Yay! Wow! I couldn't believe it. I was going to be a mommy. Me? It was an incredible feeling. I was ready to go out shopping and start buying baby clothes. I couldn't wait. My husband was so excited. He grabbed and kissed me in the doctor's office. His actions frightened me.

I looked down in the suitcase thinking to myself why did I keep all his blue booties and sweaters? There were blankets, baby rattles, toy keys, diapers, and several little outfits all tucked away. Also, in the suitcase wrapped neatly was our son's laminated birth certificate with his tiny, little footprints and my thumbprints printed on the white piece of paper.

As I re-folded his little onesies, I remembered that the experience of giving birth was like nothing that I had explored before. Labor pains were such an excruciating agony of this little baby bursting out of a tunnel too small for such a big head. I could feel my skin ripping underneath me. I was about to pass out. The time seemed to move like a turtle for my child to leave my shelter and enter the world. I actually felt like dying and then I could come back to life and cuddle my little bundle of joy.

I am not familiar with my baby's existence after I felt him leave my flesh. Only silence had entered the room. It was the only element present that made itself welcomed into my hospital room. No one had invited this thief. I was terribly broken. I was empty. I felt alone. Where did everybody go? I heard no sounds nor was there anyone there to fill the void that I suddenly felt. My womb was empty on the inside, equivalent to my empty arms on the outside. I couldn't even cry out the way the mothers had done for their first-born sons in the days of Jesus Christ's birth.

That is a day no mother ever embraces nor forgets. For me that was April 4, 1987. I never even got the chance to hold his little body or count any of his little fingers or his toes. It all was just snatched away from me. All I remember is feeling him leave me for good.

The doctors had me in a bed upside down, hoping that the gravity would keep my baby from slipping out. But this technique failed. My baby was too far down in the birth canal for anyone but God to stop his exit. He was stolen from me. I remember the medical professionals reported to me that our son did not survive because his lungs were not fully developed. The lungs are generally the last to develop in the process of an embryo developing into a fetus. My son was not quite 21 weeks developed, and he was less than a pound in weight. There was no funeral or any type of memorial for his memory. But for several years, I lit a candle on April 4 in memory of his life. I kept the candle burning all day, dedicating a prayer for protection for his soul.

Daniel Germaine Sanders would be 19 by now. His first name Daniel was Biblical like Daniel in the Old Testament. And my son's middle name Germaine from my favorite heartthrob of the Jackson 5. Daniel would have been one year older than his younger brother and five years older than his little sister.

One Sunday during a baby's Christian/Dedication in church, I dashed emotionally out of service. It was just too soon for me to celebrate for such an occasion. I couldn't even fake an apology for my heartfelt actions. The lost was too deep of a slash across my heart. Comforting arms weren't even comforting.

The nurse had asked me if I wanted to see my son. I answered no. I had carried his body inside me for five months, and now he was dead. With my vivid imagination, I did not want to go through life picturing his lifeless body and closed eyes in my intellect forever. As I filed through the suitcase, I felt emotionless as though his birth was an event that aligned with a nightmare.

But the suitcase in the attic told the true story that Daniel Germaine was once a real addition to the Sanders family.

Losing a baby must be one of the most devastating disappointments any woman has to tread through. I came to the hospital pregnant but left the hospital empty handed. There was nothing I could do to reverse what had happened to my growing child. It appeared I was sad and depressed all the time. I wanted to go down lower than I felt. My husband was brave enough to see our son's lifeless body.

Babies that are less than a pound fit in the palm of a person's hand. I actually gave birth to a live baby that weighed less than a pound. I went into labor. His body was big enough that I felt him leave the opening of my flesh. He tore out of me. But survival snuffed him out. As long as Daniel didn't survive, I didn't want to talk about him. Nor did I want to survive either.

Aside from my son's weak lungs, another explanation that was given to me was that I had a weak, incompetent cervix. I was capable of getting pregnant. There's just a chance I might not be able to hold a baby to full term. That's what happened; my cervix was too weak to hold my baby inside. Why didn't my gynecologist see that coming and do something before I lost my baby? Maybe if I had not been working and climbing those darn steps, Daniel would be alive. The doctor told me we would not know about my cervix unless I had experienced losing my baby first. In other words, that was the only way my problem could be discovered. What type of crap was that? There were no symptoms that showed him anything was wrong with my body in any of the prenatal examinations. I did not believe him, and I blamed him for not being more knowledgeable about my condition beforehand. I vowed that he would never treat me again. Ever! I was angry with him. Others agreed. With all of his exams and with technology, why didn't he see something was wrong? Too late now.

I wasn't sure how my pastor's daughter found out about my loss, but she called me and gave me her condolences then invited me to sing on the Young Adult Chorale. She was the choir director and wanted me to join, so I did. It probably was just what the doctor ordered. At my new church, singing on the choir was the first ministry I became a part of like when I was four at my old church. I didn't know anyone sitting in the alto section. But a young lady that I was told to sit next to became my first friend on the choir. I did not know at that time that she was also the daughter of the minister of music. She was very pleasant and made me feel very comfortable. I enjoyed rehearsals. It gave me a feeling of belonging to a church again. Somehow, I was placed with the funny cut up crew. My new friend's brother would always have us laughing, and then when it was interrupting rehearsals, everyone played innocent. It wasn't a party, but her brother was always the life of the rehearsal.

As much as I tried to run away from the reality of losing my child, there was no place to run to. I remember wanting to climb into a hole and disappear. I couldn't even get away from my thoughts; they kept haunting me. Trying to overcome the loss of a baby is a very traumatic experience for a mother. I was in such a bad mental cave. No, I could not change what had happened. As much as I wanted my baby back, that could not happen. But God sent me so much support once again. Music does amazing things to your heart and to your soul. Joining the choir was a way of escape for me. Singing on the choir and the fellowship started the healing process of my heart. Once again, the Lord was rescuing me.

CHAPTER 11

Just as my childhood place of worship was my first spiritual foundation and had molded my childhood, my adult place of worship was where I ended up growing more in my spirituality, spiritual education and began to branch out more in music, choir directing, theater.

After a period of time, I began occasionally directing the choir. The minister of music unexpectedly put me up to direct the choir and congregate the benediction at the end of service. When that was over, she came to tell me, "You definitely know what you are doing." But as usual, for whatever reason, there was conflict about me directing the choir that really didn't have anything to do with my ability to direct. I guess the problem with me directing the choir had to do with favoritism. No matter what anyone decided, it didn't stop me from being who I was and what God had placed inside of. This place of worship was not the most embracing place I'd been. There were inner struggles that battled with me. The majority of the folks were not warm individuals. They always had a bunch of cliques, which I hated because it singled others out of a group. It's a form of bullying. Whether a person had more education, nicer clothes, fancier car, or more money didn't make them better than others. Being a member there was a living nightmare. I had two people who were good friends of mine talk about me behind my back and then turn their backs on me during a low time of my life. Their lack of loyalty affected me in a manner they had no idea. And probably really did not care.

No matter what folks said or did not say at church, I kept busy in some type of ministry. I wanted to leave, but I stayed because I enjoyed my relationship with God. I went to Sunday School and joined the TV ministry. I became certified as an audio technician. I learned how to operate sound equipment for plays, services, and weddings. The board included 100 plus channels, speakers, and other connected equipment. Our church had a bible accredited school where I took several religious courses including two classes in the book of Revelation. I also assisted in directing two different choirs; however, because I always had to deal with chaos on the choir. In 2007, I stepped down from singing on the choir.

All I wanted to do was use my gifts and abilities for God's glory, but every church gave me a hassle on the choir. I took part in other ministries like the food and clothes bank. I was parent coordinator for the drum corp. My husband and I were married couple greeters together, welcoming everyone into the church edifice. I worked with the drama ministry assisting with sound and lighting. Not to mention, I became vice president of the disability ministry. A minister and I created this ministry to help include those living with disabilities to be included as active members of the church congregation. Unfortunately, this appeared to be a ministry that folks were against. There are bullies in the church, too. I believe several folks were uncomfortable with persons living with a disability, especially disabilities that could be seen with the eye.

My foundation of working in ministry grew at my new church as a young adult. Against many odds. I experienced so much adversity like what Jesus must have gone through with the Pharisees and Sadducees (the church folk). Here I was dealing with conflict, favoritism, and cliques in the church. Here again, I was dealing with chaos on the choir about giving me permission to direct on the choir. Why? Because I was not favored. I felt very uncomfortable as a member, but I kept on attending. God gave me several interests and talents. So, when one ministry didn't work, I worked on another. I knew who I was, and I knew my purpose. I am a praiser, and I love to hear the Word of God taught and preached. I was not there for people. I was there to glorify God with my life. I did not know people talked about others just because they didn't live where they did or didn't make the same amount of money or had the same amount of education as they did. I sure didn't know how much some church folks focused so much on materialistic stuff over God. Church politics is whack. Aren't people supposed to be attending church to have their soul fed? Attending church is supposed to be about the love of Christ. God's people are supposed to demonstrate love like Jesus did. How are people not going to feel accepted in church? But I stayed because of several reasons. My husband was there, my children were active, and I wanted to use my gifts and talents in church. I was not about to allow anyone to force me to leave. Remember, I was then, and still am, a rebel! When God knows your heart is pure, he won't allow people to keep blocking you. Church is not for flesh on parade. This is why I am so blessed today because my service to God is pure. Like the song says, "When Jesus says, yes, nobody can say no."

CHAPTER 12

What do you do when you lose a child: cry often and desire for another? Remember, we're the couple that doesn't wait long for things to happen. Once we got the medical approval to start again, we didn't hesitate. Intimacy was okay, but sometimes, it wasn't. We were trying too hard, and I needed to get over thinking I couldn't have children. Growing up, I never ever thought I would have an issue with having a baby. On top of trying, my husband was beginning to have health challenges of his own. He was diagnosed with high blood pressure and diabetes. As frustrating as it was, we kept trying. I was watching the calendar to know when I was ovulating.

When we hit it, I was pregnant for the second time. Goodbye, old doctor, you're not causing me to lose another child. They weren't doll babies. When you gave me the first urine pregnancy test you said I wasn't pregnant. Then when you gave me the second urine pregnancy test, you said I was pregnant. I couldn't trust him with the care of another life. I knew what my home pregnancy test said. I knew I was pregnant. I had symptoms similar to those of my first pregnancy. I knew my body. I agreed to taking the blood test to prove to this quack that I was pregnant. The blood test came back positive. New doctor on board. My cervix may be incompetent, but Mr. Gyn, as far as I am concerned, you are incompetent, too. Goodbye, you are the weakest link.

My girlfriend since the age of six recommended me to her cute doctor. I wanted him to take care of my baby and me. He and his staff were awesome. They were giving me tests I didn't have before. I had a conference with the new doctor and a nurse the first time I became their patient. They were my team. Despite how great they were, my appointments were not so great. Instead of gaining weight, I was losing weight. And why was my sugar going up more and more every time I had an appointment? I lost my appetite; food made me sick. All I was eating was popsicles. No wonder my sugar kept going up. Come to find out I was a gestational diabetic, so I had to be placed on a special diet.

My spiritual mother was continually asking how was the President, referring to my child inside my womb. We didn't even know whether I was carrying a boy or a girl. She was declaring and decreeing we were having a boy and that my son would be the president.

To hold onto this baby, my new doctor put me on strict bed rest. I was allowed little activities up to my due date in October of 1988. I would have to go through a whole hot summer.

We were able to move into my parents' house to help us save money. Sleeping in the basement was the best place for me being it was cool. When I lived at home, I always slept in the basement during the summer because it was always cooler down there instead of in my hot bedroom.

I didn't realize that some married people spent time alone. I was doing a lot of being alone since my husband worked two jobs. Very seldom did I see him in between jobs. We spent little time together. I was a little bored in the basement by myself. But for a great portion of the day, I would read out loud to my child, or we would listen to music. I'd place the speaker near my belly so my baby could hear the music I was listening to clearly.

I got more and more anxious about whether I was having a boy or a girl. The ultrasound technician predicted that because of my baby's fast heart rate that I was having a girl. I was sure hoping the tech was wrong. I didn't know how to do a little girl's hair. Once during a sonogram, I got scared something was wrong with the baby being the tech had a difficult time hearing our baby's heartbeat. The fear fled when I learned my little person was moving around so much the technician couldn't catch up with the heart rate. A highly active baby.

When I became about five months pregnant, I had to have surgery to close my womb and tie a surgical string around my cervix. I was actually put to sleep for this procedure to close the child inside. When I got further along, my child's weight pressed against my cervix. This is why I was instructed to be in bed and not on my feet much. It was also why I had to be sown closed. That also meant we were on lockdown for months from having physical intimacy. I also had to be cautious of all my other activities. But it didn't keep me from praising God in a dance; I just needed to be careful.

When I became pregnant this time, I had to take a temporary leave of absence from singing on the choir because it was so hot on the choir loft, I did continue working with my other ministry in the sound room. My duties basically were making copies of the church services, taking church members' orders, and keeping our sound room organized and equipped with supplies.

While we were out at dinner celebrating our two-year wedding anniversary, little busybody started kicks, flips, and somersaults inside my belly. Not to mention this child loved to ball up under my rib. I often had to pat on my belly or try to push the baby down out of my rib cage. During my whole pregnancy, I had lost less than 10 pounds. I was ready to eat, but this baby would not behave. That was not the time to be trying to pop out. Nor was I sharing my wedding anniversary every year with this child's birthday. "Little baby," I said, "October 4 is my day not yours. Do not be trying to come out today."

I guess my child decided to get me back. For four days after that, I had contractions on and off every day. Some days, I slept on my knees on the floor. A few days, I got very little sleep. By this time, my gyn doc had removed my stitches so that I could dilate. But the process was slow. I stayed at the same dilation for a day. Everything stopped happening, and I was miserable. The doctor told my husband to take me on walks, maybe that would make me dilate faster. We walked around the block and around the mall. I was tired. Plus, trying to walk 9 months pregnant was like being in mortal combat. On the evening of October 8, I sat on my chair in tears. I begged that something be done. I had already been to the hospital but was sent home due to another false alarm. This time, when my doctor brought me back in, I was told I would have the baby. But I was told I needed a good night's rest for the task that was ahead.

Everyone who wants a baby must be crazy. Who thinks about having to push a body through such a little hole while going through so much excruciating pain. Just so this person can call you "Mom." I did feel like I was about to die. I was in labor for two days. This child would start coming then change his or her mind. "I'm not coming out now, maybe later." It was brutal torture on me.

When my son was finally born with a headful of hair, the pain immediately ceased. The doctor was amazed at the grip my son had on the doctor's jacket coming out of the womb. The doctor was impressed that my son was an extraordinarily strong little guy. I guess my son was saying, "Ya not gonna drop me."

I was amazed and frightened. This little boy had some of the darkest hair; his skin was light gray with very dark pupils that were wide open looking at me like he knew me. I told the nurse to take "this baby," my own baby 'cause he was scaring me, ha! I heard that my husband's relatives questioned whether my husband was the father of our child because he was so much lighter than both of us. This shows how unintelligent some can be on genetics and family traits. My mother-in-law, two of her sisters, and two of my husband's sisters were all light skinned. My own grandfather was light skinned, and two of my siblings were light skinned also. In families, there are a variety of shades of African Americans. It didn't mean they were not blood connected. I wanted someone to question me, but they never did.

My son was named by his father and by my father. He was not the 3rd because he and his father have two different middle names. I did not approve of my husband's middle name for my son. It was a country name that sounded like it was for an old man.

I enjoyed having my own son. I enjoyed being his mom. Sleep was scarce. My son woke up every two hours to be fed. Most of my life was geared to being at home, doing things around the house, and being this little guy's mom. I didn't have a job, so I was a stay-at-a-home mom for a while.

It wasn't until my son was old enough to go to school that I found a part-time job. We were blessed to have my dad around. I was watchful and particular where and who my son was around. He was not shipped around to a lot of houses. He only went over my sister's and our parents'. Going to a day care was out of the question. Instead, his grandfather was his babysitter. Out of that, a close bond between grandfather and grandson developed.

I became a cashier at Thriftway Super Market, and learning a new job was challenging, but the head cashier was stern but patient. She kept telling me "Lynn, you're gonna get it." And I did get it, to a point that customers were looking to get in my line. They said I knew how to get them out in a timely fashion without making consumers wait in line long. My motto was why should customers have to be in a line long just because I had to be there for eight hours. During my time there, I had mastered the skills to do my job exceptionally well.

We were definitely blessed with a healthy son. There weren't too many trips to the hospital. Outside of his regular checkups, I only remember us having to take him to the hospital twice. One of the worst incidents that happened to him occurred in the church's sound room where he wanted to be with me. My son was sitting in one of the tall stools. Somehow, he fell out of the chair, and it landed on his head. He was about seven years old. The red blood would not stop coming. His shirt was covered with blood. We had to hurry him to ER. When I was told that my son needed stitches placed in his head, I excused myself out of the room to summon his father. And Mommy didn't come back. I left the room because I was afraid to watch the doctor put needles in my son's head. Why wasn't his father in the room in the first place? The next time I saw my little boy he had a big patch on his head. Then he came to me wanting some loving, which I freely gave him hugs and kisses.

This little guy of ours enjoyed church, music, and singing almost as much as the rest of our family. He was always following behind his grandfather Deacon Taylor. When my son was about 4, he was repeating my dad's popular telephone greeting, "Praise the Lord."

He was about 5 when he began singing on the children's church choir. My dad often recorded my son singing songs that he had taught him. He sure enjoyed his grandson. I guess they were having church while we were at work. When my son began going to kindergarten for half a day, I would take him in the morning, and Pop Pop picked him up at lunch time—just like my dad used to do for me when I was a little girl. Pop Pop was always doing something for one of his children or the grands. It was obvious that my father loved his family.

My son definitely was the little social butterfly in school. No matter who the teacher put him next to, that person became his buddy. He started talking when he was about six months old and had never stopped. Someone asked, "Lynda, where you get this talking baby from?" My son's teacher eventually had to put his desk next to hers away from all the other classmates. He didn't really have a behavior problem, thank God, and he also got his school work done. He just talked a lot to anybody and everybody.

Motherhood is a sacrifice. Becoming a mom became an art, an honor, and a gift to me. Even though I had several challenges throughout my pregnancy, the outcome was rewarding. I gave birth to a healthy son who was born strong.

Looking back at the past, I see so much that was prepared for my son even from the womb. I did not realize how much of my son's environment with music, singing, church, and reading to him was laying a sure foundation for his future. The time spent with my son has groomed him. No wonder he and his grandfather became buddies. They spent a lot of quality time together that was needed. Remember, my dad wanted a son when I was born. He finally got the son he wanted.

Time spent with your child or children is a period when seeds are planted, and every plant needs to grow with good ingredients. Children are nurtured just by their parents' presence and being brought up in a loving environment. That impacts them for the rest of their lives.

CHAPTER 13

In 1987, my oldest sister had a stroke caused by an aneurysm. No one expected the road that was about to come. Instead of getting better, she continued to get worse. Not missing one day, my mother patrolled down to the hospital to see the child she had given birth to before all of us. This enemy caused my sister to be placed on all types of lit machines with squiggling colored lines. It was devastating watching her in this state. My sister was no longer able to talk. The only movement that had not left was her moving her eyes, mouth, and fingers.

Why!?

Instead of wearing a necklace, a trachea had invaded her neck. This opening in her neck had to be cleaned of mucus several times a day. Otherwise, my sister would choke to death. Watching the nurses use a tube to go down my sister's throat annoyed me. She looked in pain. My sister didn't tolerate nonsense, so there's no doubt that she would have gripped up the nurse for what they were doing to her, but instead, all she could do was move her eyes and gag. With her eyes widening in size every time this procedure was done told us that she was probably in agony. My mother bought my sister a little stuffed animal to squeeze whenever she was in pain. I loved my big sister, and I despised this visit to the hospital. I hated this scene. But it wasn't about me. She needed to see us, all of us. I would sit by the side of her bed and talk to her, not knowing whether she understood a word I said or not.

After a year of being in the hospital, my sister was able to come home. We were excited but nervous at the same time. Being that I had medical background, I was going to be her caregiver, but I was concerned about the cleaning out of her trachea. This obviously was extremely uncomfortable for her. A family member asked me would I rather clean it or let her choke and die. Of course, I didn't want my sister to die, but I didn't want to inflict pain on her either.

The same week my sister was scheduled to come home, she caught pneumonia. Again, Mom did not miss one visit. One evening, when she was singing to my sister, the Lord came in, and my sister slipped quietly to her eternal rest. My mother didn't even know my sister had passed. The nurse came in the room, so intrigued by my mother's singing, and it was at that moment the nurse informed my mother that my sister had passed.

My oldest sister was my mother's first child she gave life to. The bond between them was inseparable. No matter the rough choices that my sister made for herself, those choices never changed the love my mother had for her oldest daughter. Instead, my mother continually supported and cared for my sister. Almost thirty plus years later, my mother had to watch her first baby's life slip away from her. How does anyone survive after experiencing that type of scene? I never saw my mother grieve for my sister in front of us. But I saw the strength in my mother that I had no shadow of a doubt was also in me.

CHAPTER 14

Often, it seemed like every time I was excited about starting something, I was eventually forced to quit. It was incredible how often some type of challenge would bombard me. I had just begun working on a new job. I was also back to working on my music as a pianist. I enrolled in a couple of piano courses at Philadelphia Community College. Plus, I had started back studying piano with an old music teacher of mine. I was going hard at being the next Liberace.

While loving everything I was doing, something happened. Surprise, surprise—I was pregnant. You have got to be kidding me. This was the second pregnancy that had slipped up on me. I mean just after we stopped trying to give my son a playmate, four years later, his playmate was on the way. Maybe if I slept instead of having these extra curricula after hour activities, Lynda would not pop up pregnant unexpectedly. Nobody believed that by the way, especially not me.

This pregnancy was just as challenging as the last one, if not more. I had to give up piano lessons because I couldn't get up close enough to the black and whites to bang. I also had to give up the job I had just begun to go on bedrest. Not to mention I had to be put to sleep again for that sewing up of my uterus.

I was considered a high-risk patient with gestational diabetes. My sugar levels were running high and wacky. This time, a specialist was added to help keep my child safe. I was being placed on insulin. When that doctor told me I had to prick my skin with a needle every day, I cried. I was scared. But to keep my child healthy, it was what I was forced to do. My baby was a surprise, but she or he belonged to me, and I definitely wanted her or him to survive. I was in love with my child already.

Our family outgrew my parents' basement. My son was 4, and there was another child on the way. With my husband working so often, on the day we moved into our new place, I was five months pregnant with only the assistance of three senior citizens to move our things. Everyone else had their different agendas. I remember it being so hot that day my dad became overheated and almost passed out. What a day.

I was always learning lessons as I went about life. At times, I didn't realize that I was learning how to endure and be strong on my journey. I couldn't understand why I could not have normal pregnancies like everyone else in my family. Maybe because nothing about my life was actually normal.

When my bundle of joy was ready to join my journey, I found myself in the hallway of our home, pacing. My husband appeared to be moving like a snail, and I had to light a fire up under him to get us to the hospital.

As soon as my stitches were snipped, I immediately went straight to 5 cm. I must have been delirious because I kept saying take my glasses off. But it wasn't my glasses I had on. It was the oxygen tube they had given me that I was feeling because my bronchitis decided to flare up. I had not had a breathing episode in years, but now, I was having breathing challenges. Some lady in labor in another room was cussing up a storm. I understood her dilemma, but I preferred calling on the name of Jesus who had the power I now needed.

No matter how old I get, that day was definitely an experience to remember. One thing after another happened. The stirrups attached to the table where women have to get into position to deliver her child were placed in backwards. The doctor tried numerous times to place it correctly, but he failed at getting the stirrup right. That metal contraption squeezed my thighs so painfully. I remember thinking, Wasn't I experiencing enough discomfort with contractions drawing near and near. Initially, the medical staff was unable to locate the anesthesiologist, but she did finally come just in the nick of time because at 5 cm my little darling popped out. This baby girl refused to wait until I was fully dilated at 10 cm like she was supposed. So impatient! Always making her own rules. The doctor literally had to catch my daughter as if she were a football. Otherwise, her little butt would have been on the floor. She busted out of me at 5cm, tearing me in three places as she exited. There was no pain when the doctor stitched me up, but I felt every pull that he made with the surgical thread.

November 11, 1992, my 6 lb. 5 oz. Mini Me arrived on Veteran's Day. My daughter slept through the night, but if I left the room, she woke up. So, I had to take my naps at the same time she took hers. She knew. This little girl was a piece of work from her conception even in the womb. She was my challenge almost in every aspect of the word. My daughter purposely kept falling out of her playpen because she didn't liked being confined. We decided we better stop putting her inside the playpen before she broke her neck. She had pink eye at least three times. One of those times her father got it, too, from her lying next to me on his side of the bed.

That little girl was my busiest child. Her brother was a deep, creative thinker. His sister changed the house. One evening, my son came upstairs screaming with his eye glued shut. While watching TV, she decided to put fingernail polish in her brother's eye. I have no idea why. Maybe he was ignoring her. Who knows. While he cried and screamed, I had to flush his eye out with warm water.

We had more hospital visits when she came along. One year, she burnt her arm climbing up on a chair and reaching over the stove for something to eat in the cabinet. She cut the palm of her hand running with a glass bottle; blood was everywhere. Her hand had to be numbed before her hand could be free from glass. Then another year, she broke that same arm, thinking she was going to make me miss Hezekiah Walker's concert at our church. I took her to the hospital *after* the concert. Another time, she cut off her eyebrow with a pair of scissors.

Just as aspirating as things could be with my daughter, she could be the most caring and loving little girl. The neighborhood children loved her. They always crowded on our steps to play with her and her little stove and kitchen set.

I remember praying that the Lord would not only equip me to be a good mother but to be the right mother for these two children. Just being any type of mother for your individual child is not always enough. Each child is different—and even more so when one is a girl and the other is a boy. My daughter was definitely different from my son, so I needed God's guidance to equip and package me with the right tools to parent them individually. And God was answering my prayer.

CHAPTER 15

Several things were going on and changing for me and my family in 1998. My husband and I were sitting in a neurologist's office that had been recommended by another specialist. What had been found was a tumor about the size of a dime that was growing on the outside of my husband's brain. The doctor said it was good that he went to his appointment to see the specialist when he did. Surgery was critical.

There would be two doctors operating, a neurosurgeon and an otolaryngologist. Some of our relatives on both sides of the family sat with me at the hospital. The procedure took about five hours. The tumor had been successfully removed, and it was not cancerous. Once out of recovery, my husband complained of an excruciating headache. The doctors had expected him to have some pain but nothing like what he was experiencing. Air pockets that had developed during surgery in his brain had to be closed. The medical staff had both his arm restrained to the bed. He was trying to pull tubes out of his flesh. He was in a desperately aggressive state of mind. The hospital performed tests after tests. My husband was acting out due to a spinal tap placed in his back. He had to be sedated to be kept still and quiet. I couldn't believe after just a few days he would have to endure a second procedure to his head. It wasn't my body, but he was my husband, and I was scared.

During surgery, first, fatty tissues were removed out of his belly. Second, the fatty tissues were used to patch up the air pockets that were giving my husband a monstrous headache. That action had nothing to do with the second procedure that had to be executed. Two procedures on one head when all he was supposed to have had was one.

After a week, my husband was discharged from the hospital. He was taken to my parents' home in an ambulance. Mom and Dad moved out of their bedroom and into the middle room so that my husband could temporarily stay at their home while he recovered. My mother owned a hospital bed in their bedroom from her previous illness. My husband had lost a lot of weight. He was a bit frail and could not stand up alone. He still had a bandage wrapped around the top of his head. Someone had to assist him to walk around the bedroom, or he would have been on the floor. We had to hold this six-footer up by his waist. A physical therapist came to the house a few times a week to help strengthen his muscles and to usher him back on track. He couldn't be left alone. We had to help him do everything. Thank God the second procedure had been a success.

During this time, I had stopped writing stories. I was overwhelmed with being a caregiver and administering meds. Maybe the Lord had given me a medical background because of my husband and my daughter always needing some type of medical care. I was, however, able to journal about my husband's sicknesses and take pictures of his daily progress. One day, he would be able to look back at his miraculous journey.

After a few days had passed, my husband began to do quite a bit of sniffling. After all he had been through, he sure didn't need to catch a cold now. What concerned me the most was he stated that the drip from his nostrils tasted salty. I didn't want to think the worst. But I sure felt in my gut that this was not supposed to be happening. I doubted that he had a cold. It was a Sunday morning when I called our church and asked to speak to one of the elders. I explained what was going on and asked for prayer. I was told later that he had the whole church praying. In the meantime, I had called the neurologist that had performed the two surgeries. Monday morning, my sister and I were back at the hospital with my husband. My husband's nasal drip had been evaluated. He would have to be readmitted. The nurse assisting the surgeon spent a lot of time explaining this situation to us. She said that in all the seventeen plus years that she had worked as a nurse, she had never seen a scenario like my husband's case.

None of us could believe that my husband needed a third surgery. I was not in his head, but I knew he was afraid. I was, too. I couldn't understand why all this was happening, and I was trying to grasp a hold of the situation. The doctors were baffled, but they knew for certain my husband needed work on his brain again. What was God saying that He wanted us to learn? We called on him relentlessly. Whatever the lesson, we did learn that my husband had a CSF leak. Brain fluid was leaking from his 'brain. That was why the liquid from his nostrils tasted salty. This was *not* normal. *This* was a living nightmare. What was happening!?

There were tears in my husband's eyes, but he didn't verbalize his feelings or his thoughts. His tears spoke loud and clear.

In the next procedure, the surgeon went in my husband's belly again but on the opposite side this time, removing more fatty issue. This time, packing went up in his nostrils. I could barely take it. This cycle had to stop. How much could one person bear and live? What state of mind was this going to put my husband in? Would he be made whole again?

It was incidents like these that thrust me into journaling. I had stopped being able to write or even think clearly. I felt like a zombie. It was as though my mind was slipping away. I was overwhelmed and emotionally exhausted. I learnt whenever I stopped completely writing in my life, those were the times I felt crazy. Writing kept my thoughts in order. Writing was therapeutic for me and a large portion of my survival kit. It was a major healing component for Lynda.

Ruth's Miracle Child
1999
By Lynda Joice

I desire to please God
Yet I feel that I don't quite measure up
The places I go. The people I see.
They all seem to have the same view of me.
No one knows that my weaknesses inside
Orchestrate the way I perform on the outside
I struggle with myself trying to do what is best
But oftentimes I feel I don't pass people's test
I look at my life.

What have I accomplished? ----not much
Am I a failure? I say yes.
The man in my life thinks so, too
But my DADDY-LORD tells me "No."
He doesn't make junk
Just give me time 'cause you I have blessed.'
I am the one that created you before I took
my rest

Yes, Lord, you have made me a puzzle
And I just don't fit
It's because I have been placed
Among the wrong 99 pieces
You listen here now, keep a stiff upper lip
God does not make any kinds of mistakes
Should I cry? For what? What changes does
that make?

Can you take a life that is not yours to take?
Hush your face! You are not allowed to usher
in
That kind of fate.
Okay DADDY, You always win
The reward you have for me is better than a
minute of sin.

God's healing power was definitely viewed and tasted upon in our home. Miracles of healing were evident. I can't say I understood why I experienced everything I did. Some things I could not articulate. Things were chaotic. I knew I had to trust God for my life, our lives, and for my family's overall well-being.

My husband was not able to work. Our finances were kicking us in the neck. How do you trust God when you can't even trace what is going on? It's not the asking how to do things that is the biggest challenge. It's more of trying to learn to do stuff without receiving answers and trying to move forward. It's walking by faith regardless of what you see or how you feel.

Some people did not understand me. I didn't always understand myself. But here was another battle where I was learning myself better. I was learning what was inside of me and learning more about my Holy God. My relationship with Him was being tested. I wasn't able to talk to everyone. I had come to stop trusting people for several different reasons. I had gotten help from the church before, but when I was told that the help I got was because of the person that helped me, I was done. I thought they were acting out of the goodness of their heart. That caused me to put an end to the friendship. Not to mention, I was constantly asked how I would pay things back once I got the help. I didn't know how, so I never asked again. I learned to stop seeking people for help but to draw closer to seeking God. Folks can be fickle. I knew how to be loyal, but folks were not loyal to me.

Quitting sometimes is exactly what people are waiting for us to do. They are stalking on social media, up close and personal. Betting and counting on you to die. Quitting is easier than standing and fighting. The best type of deliverance I learned was getting delivered from people. I embraced being a Lone Ranger. I had to get delivered from how people rejected me and delivered from their opinions of what they said about how I was propelling from my pain. As important as it is to know that there are people out there waiting on us to quit, there are just as much, if not more, people needing us to carry on. We're needed! It's exactly why so many of us were born—to make a tremendous positive impact in this world. We are a part of this gracious, great generation. And equally why our enemy of this world comes to distract and feed us lies. He even uses our own flesh against us.

Poems by Lynda Joice

2000
I See Your True Colors

Don't tell me you love me
I've already seen your rejection signs
You only show your hate and a pocketful of lies.
I rather you remove the mask from your faces.
Don't you realize the ones you wear are like transparent vases?

I see you better than you can see me
You're only a fake, a doll made of plastic,
Playing house and pretending to be great!

March 2000
With All My Heart

I will not accept defeat for my life.
The holes that you dig for me they are just
not big enough.
The holes that you dig for me I will take them
in stride.
You wonder why—because the Lord is filling
my cup.
I've decided to fight
You with all of my might in spite.
I tell myself daily,
Don't believe the hype
God has ordained success for me.
He has engraved it in gold.
So I am telling you that you have no choice.
You have to, and you will release your hold!

June 2000
Are Angels Real?

Yes, there are real
Do angels walk the earth?
Yes, they do, they are not very far.
I know what you are thinking
I know you're laughing at me
I hear you saying in your mind
What in the world is that woman smoking or
drinking?

But I can prove to you this day
I am not crazy
I no longer do drugs
Just listen to what I have to say.
God gave us an angel
Sometimes rather soft spoken
She sings under the anointing
With a heart of gold
When others are in need
Her humble heart sure does bleed
Have you guessed it yet?
Who is the person you have in mind?
If you know her like I do
You'll agree my sister is one of a kind.

In 2001, I was on the job at the YMCA as their music coordinator. They had several programs, but they did not offer any music programs. I created the first Abington YMCA music program for their day care. This program catered to children from babies to 5-year-olds. I made up lyrics to nursery rhymes accompanied by music. Everyone loves to dance and shake their bootang. I taught musical games that were fun and educational. The Y allowed me to order a tape recorder, supplies, musical tapes, and musical instruments, so the children really had a ball with me. The babies would laugh, grin, and move their arms and feet. The older children played the musical instruments. The children knew when it was time for me to entertain, and they were excited when I arrived. When it was time for the five-year-olds to graduate, I was appointed to run and organize their graduation. Because of my impressive job performance at work, I was promoted to be assistant coordinator for the day care. I was no longer doing music. Instead, I became a team leader over most of the employees working in that department. Let me tell you, everyone was not happy about that change, and I don't mean just the children. Folks felt intimidated by my position. A new supervisor and a new teacher put their heads together to set me up, and like always, others' deception landed me out of job. A month later, I heard that the new supervisor was fired. A person will reap what they sow, good or bad.

My son was in junior high school and living in the suburbs with my sister and her family. I was very much against my son going to any neighborhood junior high school in Philly. It was hard not seeing him every day. We only saw him on Wednesdays for bible class and on the weekends. It didn't matter that he was with family. He still was separated from his immediate family during the week. The decision was for his best interest in regard to his safety and for his education, but I felt guilty as if I were abandoning my son. I was happy to go pick him up on Fridays but sad to take him back on Sundays. My heart would break then every time.

We had, despite circumstances, fallen into a routine in our lives, but a couple weeks into 2001, on Wednesday, January 17, that routine of life changed. I picked up my son from my sister's for bible class. My husband said he was unable to pick our daughter up because he wasn't feeling well. He wanted me to ask my parents if they could get my daughter from school. They did.

That evening, my family was gathered together in that crowded hospital's emergency waiting room with numerous faces of various colors. The unpleasant smell of disinfectant and sweat mixed together, shooting through the nostrils of patients and visitors alike. It was well after one o'clock a.m. when doctors came and told me news I did not want to hear.

"What do you mean my husband won't make it through the night!?" I was startled. Those words made my skin crawl; I thought I was about to vomit. Hearing that horrific sentence gripped my heart. The tall pale-faced doctor who was in charge of ER had just spoken a death verdict over my husband. Like a snake, his words struck, seeping their venom into me. Silently in my spirit, I said, *"So what he's a doctor. He's not GOD. He may be in charge here, but he's not in charge of life. How dare he say such a deadly thing to me?"*

I automatically blurted out a rebuttal to his declaration of death that must have come from the Holy Ghost. I immediately spoke life: "Yes, he will make it through the night."

I'd heard those words so loud and clear in the balance of my hearing, but I was astonished at how the words had come out of my own mouth with such strong conviction. I did not recall rehearsing the thought. The words just automatically jumped out my mouth.

I stood alongside my mother-in-law, witnessing the tears streaming down her full face. I was annoyed that she was shedding tears. She was acting as though her son's life was already snuffed out of him. Who gave out the memo that there would be a body for the funeral director or morgue to collect that night? **No weapon formed against my husband will prosper.**

Again, we faced a moment that seemed like an interruption. It was an unwanted invasion on our privacy. My husband was lying up in the emergency room with a 500-sugar reading. His blood pressure number on top was over 200. He was unconscious, running an uncontrollably high fever. Though my husband was unconscious since the moment he was found in our daughter's bedroom chair, no one knew what his diagnosis was. My husband presented himself as a puzzle to the medical staff. Hours of confusion taunted our minds. No one could figure out the mystery. Medical attendants kept sprinting in and out of the small cubicle where my husband lie unconscious. Technology screens all around the room beeped with visual colorful squiggly lines running across them. Time was ticking, and no matter what treatment was performed, my husband would not wake up. Terror was running rampant. A tube had to be administered in his veins because he was periodically vomiting, causing him to lose fluids. Immediate antibiotic medication was administered through an IV in an attempt to bring down the life-threatening fever he carried, and medication also had to be given for the spontaneous way he was vomiting up fluids.

I stood over my husband praying while watching him sweat profusely. I could cry and accept defeat over my husband's dilemma. Instead, I had to think, speak, and have faith while constantly knowing that "You shall live and not die."

I couldn't break down in front of everyone, even though fear bombarded my thoughts. I suddenly walked out the room with my mother and my sisters on my heels. I blurted out that this was a nightmare that couldn't possibly be intruding on us once again. They tried comforting me, but my mind kept racing.

Lord, when is this nightmare going to end? Lord, we can't go through this again. He had just recovered from three emergency brain surgeries just two years ago. His head just can't take anymore.

Though I tried to fight it, I relived the moment that led us to this hospital.

I had our children in the car, and I pulled up in front of our house at about 6:30 p.m. to let them go inside out of the cold. The neighborhood was quiet and dark. I navigated the car down the block to find a parking space. I was not even down the street fully before my daughter and son dashed toward the car, screaming, "Mommy, something is wrong with Daddy. He doesn't look right."

What did that mean: "he doesn't look right"? He had looked fine this morning before I left for work, and he sounded fine during our conversation over the telephone. He did say he felt ill that he must be getting the flu. He said he was experiencing a headache and was vomiting. My husband was planning to follow up with bed rest. I decided on the way home I'd stop at the market to get him some juices.

Inside our 9-year-old daughter's bedroom, she had found him seated in a chair, partially undressed, with his eyeballs rolling to the back of his head. Perspiration poured out of his pores. His skin felt wet and clammy. Saliva rolled down the side of his mouth. My daughter hysterically jumped around while my son stood frozen in place with a horrific expression on his face.

My past experience in nursing automatically kicked in. Principles and techniques rose out that had been living dormant inside of brainwaves. I found myself performing medical procedures over this dead weight man. My husband's body felt hotter than July. He was burning up. It was as though hell was present in the room.

I looked into my son's terrified eyes. "Son, I need you to be a big boy." I instructed him to call 911 and to take care of his little sister.

My son took my daughter out of the room, but I never left the room for fear my husband would die if I withdrew my presence away from him. If he did not need me, we needed him to survive. Life would never be the same without the man who vowed to be my lifelong partner. I expected us to watch our children graduate from junior high school, high school and, one day, college together. Our daughter would need her dad to give her away one day in marriage, and our 13-year-old son needed his father to show him how to be a man.

The paramedics asked 1,000 questions. "No, my husband doesn't take drugs!" That was an absurd thought. And the question annoyed me. They were trying to insinuate that he might have tried to commit suicide by taking an overdose of drugs. I did not care if they needed to ask or not. The answer was, "No and stop asking!"

Day after day, family members sat in the hospital baffled without a diagnosis. And during those days, my husband remained in a coma. I spent hours in the hospital, even slept there all night. I was exhausted most of the time, and I barely ate. I had no appetite. The family hung on by the grace of God. He was not dead. He had made it **through** that first night versus what the ER doctor had stated. God was not a man that He would lie.

Telephone calls were coming from New York, North Carolina, and Virginia with words of encouragement and prayers. Each day, I kept things normal for my children, driving them to their activities. They still needed one of their parents. I didn't want them to experience the turmoil.

On the flip side, who was holding me together? Who was carrying me? Who was holding me up so that I didn't fall apart? I was operating as though I was on another planet. I was there, but I wasn't there. The weight of uncertainty hovered over me. I felt numb and lethargic most of the time. People saw my smile, but it wasn't real. Others may have saw the truth behind my dreamy eyes. Many felt I was portraying a woman of strength, but I felt like a basket case, broken and crumbling into pieces.

It took three days before the doctor's diagnosis; my husband had bacterial meningitis. The Board of Health was notified.

They called. I spoke with them on the wire. My husband's present place of employment was put on alert. Calls were coming to me left and right with questions. All I wanted was to be hidden from this agony. Inquiring minds were investigating where or who my husband could have contracted such a death sentence from. This usually wipes people off of the planet. How could my husband still be alive with such a murderous, monstrous attack to his body?

Everyone who lived in our house was given a huge white antibiotic horse pill. The tablet was to protect us from being affected from past, present, and future contamination of meningitis. Fear was felt through every relative in the packed hospital halls. They sort of wanted to shy away from us and treat us like the plague.

Meningitis is a villain that kills or destroys hearing, extremities, and other operations of a human being. It is an infection to the brain. The symptoms vary from stiff neck, headache, fever, vomiting, or other similar flulike symptoms. It can be highly contagious. It can be transmitted from close contact with a person, drinking behind someone, or using the same utensils belonging to an effected individual. The possibilities are large and can very well be fatal.

How the disease took hold of our household was a mystery. My husband stayed in a coma for days. Every night, I played "Jehovah Jireh you are more than enough" in his ears. The Holy Ghost led me to read Psalms 6 one evening before leaving him still in a comatose state. When I came back the very next morning, he was sitting straight up, head bandaged, eyes wide open, acknowledging and verbalizing that I was his wife. I was amazed and ready to do the Holy Dance. The nurse threatened if I did not pipe down, I'd have to leave the hospital. She didn't understand how happy I was to have him recognize and acknowledge me. I have been a praiser since I was filled with the Holy Ghost in high school. I am an atmosphere changer by right. I danced pregnant. I grunted. "Whatever! Let him try to put me out of this hospital after days of facing closed eyes that only God could open." I wasn't going anywhere. They would have to get an army to escort me out of the building. The male nurse was speaking from a medical perspective, but he had not endured the dark days we had traveled down the past week.

My husband woke up excited, talking about he couldn't wait to watch the Super Bowl. Sorry, sir, but you missed that. He couldn't believe that he had missed the game due to being in a coma. He did not realize he had missed several days of his life. Then those in the room were baffled why he would not follow the medical staff's instructions. He wasn't weak. His strength had returned. But my concern was the expressions of confusion plastered upon his face when we spoke to him. We would ask him questions or give him directions, but he just stared at us quietly, not following directions. He didn't even try to attempt. Then I was the one who discerned something was wrong. I heard the Lord tell me that my husband could not hear. I didn't realize at the time the impact that would play out. Just like the Lord told me the week before in my ears that "Your husband cannot take care of you. I will take care of you." God was speaking to me again. Then two days later after that, my husband had slipped into a coma.

Not once did my husband cry out, "I can't hear!" He just kept quiet. He was confused by what was going on around him. He did not realize that he had awaken to a world of silence. My husband was deaf. I was shocked; I couldn't believe that this was' some horrible nightmare. I remember the social worker sharing with me she'd be in tears if a barrier like this came between her and her husband to keep them from being able to communicate. I could not explain how I felt about being robbed of something that belonged to us.

Life had flipped upside down. We all were often frustrated trying to communicate with a deaf family member. People that didn't live with us didn't understand that we were a family of three most of the time, but there were four of us living under one roof. My husband often distanced himself from us. It was not my intention to be married but still single. My children had an absentee father that they only saw with the eye. He was not engaging with them. This was not something either of us had bargained for. I no longer recognized the man whom I was married to. The situation was very much like living with a stranger. He just wasn't there.

We couldn't use sign language. We tried to learn, but that didn't work. My husband tried reading lips, but he was very poor at comprehending. Most of the time, he didn't understand what was being said to him, and because of this, we didn't communicate—not verbally anyway. We tried so may techniques, but my husband would quit. He often verbalized they were too hard. We began to text more via cell phone and write things down to communicate. Things had traumatically changed in our home.

Many hearing equipment and tools that have been exercised, including the cochlear implant, had failed. He regretted ever having the implant done. The device had not changed his silent circumstance. Things that had worked for others did not work for him. He lived in a silent world day after day, frustrated, angry, and distant from us and the world.

What do you do when all fails? I wrote my prayers out. We learned to hold on to "All things work together for the good for those that are the called...." Through tears, we exercised, "Oh magnify the Lord with me and let us exalt His name together." I still exercise in difficult times, standing on the promises of God and to walk by faith and not by sight. I remind God that it is written "I've never seen the righteous forsaken nor His seed begging for bread." We are taught to meditate on God's word. We are taught that the trying of your faith works patience, and faith without works is dead. We are also taught that trouble don't last always. And, yes, we do run out of patience. And, yes, God does allow us to go down some horrible roads that aren't a bed of roses. And many things are not fair. And many times, we also do hurt on the inside. I call it "the Joseph/Job experience." Joseph and I have so many things in common. We are both the youngest in the family. We both were put in pits but different types. We were both taunted by someone to have an inappropriate sexual encounter with them. And we both were dreamers.

Truth be told, all that teaching looks and feels different when you have to face difficult realities. Then, I go into my bag of outlets. Sometimes, they are done through tears, breathing techniques, and affirmations. Learn to speak well of yourself. Love on yourself. After spending some time crying, use your outlet. Find a happy place. Sometimes, for me, it was going to the gym or exercising. That is how we fight the good fight of faith. Get up and fight depression. Tell it to leave.

As far as I was concerned, with all the struggles that we had gone through in our lives, there's nothing like being a child of the King. I'm grateful that God chose to love me. I'm grateful to be on the winning side. Even though we had dealt with a lot of hell on Earth, there were others who would not be able to stand where my husband and I had stood.

Nope, I never asked for these experiences. Some I did question, but through it all, I had learned about me. I was then, and still am, an amazing, resilient woman. Did these things hurt? You darn skippy they did.

In spite of things happening in my life, I am still in my right mind. Even though there was a time doctors wanted to medicate me for depression, I told them, nope, not happening. Not having anything controlling my mind and emotions. I got too much in life that God has appointed for me to do to be doped up on meds. I told the therapist, "Whatever is going on with me, it is nothing that God can't help me fix."

Lynda Joice

Poem by Lynda J.

I'm a big bad soldier
Ready to fight
Here is my Bible
To teach me to walk right
When I get my praise on
Then I will shout, "Jesus is with me"
You better watch out and learn to fight!

CHAPTER 16

My children were school age, so it was time for me to become a full-time employee. I became connected to a school district that was more of a professional, educational setting. This time, I was hired in a suburb school district outside of Philadelphia as a one-on-one under the umbrella of being a para-professional for students with behavioral and learning disabilities. Working with students who had disabilities was new for me. I wasn't just assisting students in the educational aspect, but other students often came to me about their intimate relationships and sometimes advice about their home environment. Youth of all ages gravitated to me, and advocating for them became my brand.

My professional assignments consisted of me shadowing a student to their learning settings. I kept communication active with everyone on the team including the student's parents. There were meetings I would have to attend with teachers, principals, and speech and behavioral specialists. Once I got to know my student, I implemented several strategies to help them meet their goals of success. I reached this expertise through observation, studying, and prayer. The most challenging student I ever had was a fifth-grade girl who was a thief with a criminal record. She stole anything in school that wasn't hers. She was a bully and a liar. There was a time she tried to threaten and intimidate me by jumping at me. I was like, little girl, if you knew me, you wouldn't do that. The Lord must have answered my unspoken prayer because she moved out of the state. Won't HE do it!?

My last student was autistic and a computer whiz. My assignment lasted with him from 5th to 12th grade. He was extremely intelligent with an amazing mind for computers and making movies. He could act and learn script lines amazingly well. Very repetitive with movie scenes. However, he wasn't good with logic, and some triggers caused him to get angry and bite. During that time, he would become extremely strong and sometimes needed to be restrained. He only hurt me twice. My wrist got bent. Then once he calmed down, he was very voluntarily apologetic. My coworkers called him my son. But he was my buddy. There's no doubt that I made a tremendous difference in his life. His parents, family, and educational professors agreed.

There can be so many talents and gifts inside of you that may be hidden. How will you know if you never try to discover them? For example, I didn't know how important I was to students that had learning disabilities. I didn't have specific training with disabilities. But I took the time to learn the student that was assigned to me. I observed their behavior and triggers. I read up on their background. I read different types of resources, and I asked other teachers and colleagues questions. Nothing that I have learned over the years has not been wasted. I got on the job training as well. I gained new knowledge and more skills. When a person gives up on themselves or doesn't know of their capabilities, someone loses out. And they can very well lose out on themselves. Someone needs you, and it could very well be yourself.

CHAPTER 17

I believe there was a period of time in my life that I blacked out. Emotionally, something appeared to had shifted inside of me that was confusing. I was just so disappointed and sad often. There were moments in my life that I could not remember. For example, I had forgotten for years that I had been molested until I was discussing some things in therapy that were brought back to memory.

I have attended therapy three times in my life. Once as a child. Twice as an adult. I also received assistance from a coach that taught different breathing techniques and meditation. I have other different coping mechanisms through line dance and going to LA Fitness.

Depression was always the culprit. Even if the root was something different. What triggered most of my mood swings of sadness came from some type of incident like how someone treated me or a negative thought that danced in my head trying to make me its dance partner. I knew logically that I was loved, but there could be a disconnect that made me feel that people didn't like or love me. Especially if they suddenly changed toward me for no reason. Feeling alone seemed to always come back. I could be in a crowded room and still feel so uncomfortable and alone. It wasn't always that people disliked me. But the thoughts in my mind often made me feel that way and that I didn't fit in. Negative thoughts spoke loud to me of rejection. I was an introvert dealing with depression. I got sick of being asked if I wanted to hurt myself. No! I wanted to live. I just wanted to stop being alone all the time. I wanted to stop hurting and having a broken heart. It was like I would receive something I wanted, and then it would be snatched from me.

Therapy often rescued me. It was as though I were releasing something horrible growing and biting me inside. I learned how to build and develop outlets that interested me. I yearned for peace of mind. One of my outlets was teaching elementary piano for a period of time. The music director believed in me and hired me just from a phone conversation. I couldn't stay working there for as long as I wanted to because the place did not have substantial heat. My body just was not conditioned to handling those low temperatures.

Some months later, an outlet was given to me that was very therapeutic for me. A young minister that I became good friends with asked me to be his assistant director for his production company. This happened just through another conversation. I was sharing with him what abilities I had in music and in the arts. It wasn't long after we were preparing for productions in rehearsals. We took his production around Philadelphia, Reading, New York, and then ATL.

Ministers or prophets that I did not know personally were forever giving me prophecies about me for as long as I could remember. Once a minister told me I would no longer be sitting in the back. God was going to elevate me. I wasn't sure what that statement meant. The guest minister took me by the hand and placed me on the front row in the church's sanctuary. There were over 500 pairs of eyes watching. I was so embarrassed as this was done in front of the whole congregation. I wasn't one for being put on the spot.

I will say being an assistant director of someone's production company was a good experience. That brought me out of my comfort zone. There was a great confidence that birthed inside of me. I saw me in action, and I was surprised by the person who had been hiding behind the scenes. It was amazing, and it opened wide a new door for me.

In 2003, after we had completed the performance in Reading, PA, we introduced the cast and staff. This practice was nothing new. The director that I worked with then called me out on stage. He began talking about the production company I would have. I knew he was wrong. My children looked at me, wondering what this man was talking about. I publicly corrected him that he must have meant that I was self-publishing a book. He publicly repeated that I would have a production company. I was puzzled. I never entertained the thought of having a production company in my life. That would be too farfetched for me to accomplish. I had worked with others doing school plays since I was a child. I wrote novels. When I started writing stories in play form, I never planned to actually perform any plays I wrote. But God had a plan for me, and he had been setting me up since I was a little girl. No wonder I couldn't figure out which one thing I wanted to do. God had placed more than one gift inside of me. Gifts that would be used in several capacities.

So guess what? In 2005, my first production under my leadership was performed titled "Deliverance" for our 6 a.m. prayer group's retreat. I pulled a few young people together, and we started practicing in my living room. The first rehearsal we had no one left until after 1 a.m. We went from having rehearsal into worship, prophecy, and getting slain in the spirit. The Holy Ghost unexpectedly came through and sat on each of us.

Everyone who agreed to be a part was faithful to learning their lines. The costumes were simple. We used black capes and white tee shirts. The day of the performance, for about 20 minutes, we had the eyes and attention of several men and women. I was astonished at the standing ovation we received at the end. The men stood first. Wow. It's something when a production ministers to a room full of men. I was told by one of the ministers how profound the message was and that we didn't take a long time to get to the point. Amen. From that day, The Vision Productions Inc. was birthed. I got the name from the scripture Habakkuk 2:2, 3: "Write the Vision, make it plain...so he may run who reads it...for the Vision awaits its appointed time...it will not lie. If it seems slow, wait for it, it will surely come, it will not delay."

Those suicidal thoughts that I once had returned in 2007. I needed to pour myself into my outlets to distract the triggers. This was the other reason I had previously decided to quit the choir. I just didn't believe there should always be so much confusion when a person needs God more than anything. So, during this time, I began writing blogs on social media. I enrolled in a creative writing class and I also became rather busy with working with the TV ministry at church. I was not new to operating a camera nor was I new to writing. But I was expanding in these two areas that I loved. They were definitely outlets that I imparted from and gave my time to. What is the point in doing anything that you volunteer to do that is not enjoyable? I even joined a meet-up writing group that gathered once a month. This group gave members the opportunity to submit literary work that could be critiqued by other writers. I stepped out on a limb feeling rather confident about submitting a play I wrote titled "One Touch from the Master." The play was about five women who were going to therapy: a crackhead, a woman with AIDS, another dealing with domestic violence, another dealing with depression, and a fallen actress. Their therapist was a Christian woman who worked for a boss that was angry with God. This therapist was trying to help everyone but lacking in her own life. Then with all the turmoil in her life, she was working for a man who was only in the mental health business for the money. My facilitator of the meet-up writing group looked down on my script. He didn't view it as believable. Did I mention that the production the facilitator had looked down on, "One Touch from the Master," was performed five times? Four of those performances were back by popular demand and performed twice in theaters. The last time we performed this production the late Erica E. Hillyard played the crackhead. Before losing Erica, we made a poster and made copies of her curled up on the stage floor playing the role of a strung-out crackhead. That picture of her on the floor has become famous. That production has been a huge success in spite of someone not believing in my work. Sometimes, we can't listen to other people. Instead, it's better to believe in yourself, believe in your own work, and step out on faith. That is why I am a dreamer who developed into a visionary. I was told many years later that my gift would make room for me. So, in spite of obstacles that I faced, I kept trying to work the gifts and the talents that have been placed inside of me.

Dreaming is something I did often. I would have a dream and create a story out of it. I have considered turning some into movies. I often wondered if my dreams were warnings. These dreams projected me into purchasing a dream book. I've had dreams of dogs, death, falling, and my teeth coming out. I dream so often that I eventually discovered that I had the gift of dreams. But I cannot interpret my dreams. I look back on my childhood now, realizing that this gift has been active in me for years. I just wasn't aware of it until adulthood. My mother shared that anytime she dreamt about someone who was deceased, she would tell them in her dream not to touch her. My mom believed that if they touched her, she would no longer be a living being.

Right before my minister/friend told me that I would have a production company, I had a rather mysterious dream. Not giving any details of my dream, I asked one of the evangelists at my old church could having dreams be a gift. She told me yes and revealed to me that she knew I had a dream recently of a murder. Yep, that was the mysterious dream that I had, and I had turned it into a story titled "Weapons."

I believed the dream was connected to my marriage. Not that anyone would be murdered. I believed it confirmed the ending of my marriage. See, when you ask God questions, He will answer—by any means. I'd learned God spoke to me through dreams and spoke no matter what I experienced, what I felt, or what I saw. I was learning that hearing His voice was a major key to my journey in life. As difficult as my journey had been, He continued to tell me to trust Him. It is so beneficial to learn who you are. That way no matter what others say, you will believe in yourself and work your gifts, talents, and dreams.

A few blogs written by Lynda Joice

Stuck in the Middle!

Since 2007, the activities of my life have flipped as much as a gymnast practicing for the Summer Olympics. Now folks are talking about some recession. My son and I were laughing, saying our family has already been in a recession for years. We wouldn't know the difference. Last week, our lights got turned off. People keep coming to our house wanting to shut some utility off. Last year, after my daughter was tarrying for the Holy Ghost, she got staph, a fatal disease. Her face blew up so bad she looked deformed. It must have been pretty fatal because her doctor kept calling my house checking on her. I just kept anointing my baby. I had to stay up to 4 a.m., washing every article of clothing and sterilized the whole house. And a few months later, my son was held at gunpoint on New Year's Eve on his way to church. They just wanted his new iPhone, not his life. You think I would learn my lesson and go somewhere and sit down and let the enemy win. But I ain't about to let the devil think he won anything. I keep listening to the voice of the Lord to do ministry. God wants all of my gifts to come forth. But I've never shared my writing until two years ago. Now, I have so many distractions that want to eat me alive and have me for breakfast. New things going on in my body now that I never had before. Someone has asked me, ever since I tried to self-publish and failed, if I was ready for this fight. I had no idea what they were warning me for. I was told that a huge demon was against my book coming out because the enemy feared the deliverance that would follow in individual lives once they read my written project. I must be awfully close to my breakthrough 'cause with the power of the Holy Ghost, I plan to blow as much of the enemy's camp up as I can. He seems to know more about what has been placed inside of me than I do.

Just a Friendly Reminder

While sitting in my gold Forenza, idled, many thoughts came rushing to my psyche. Some of the thoughts were welcomed, but others were like unwelcomed house guests. I'm often reminded how my pastor's wife once told me in her office that she felt I was a deep thinker. Sometimes thinking that deep over stuff you don't even want to think about can be rather annoying. The thing about it, I can't help it. That is just a part of who I am. I also believe that is a part of the artistic, imaginary side of me. Then someone probably is wondering what in the world are you doing sitting in the car for naught anyway. Well sitting in my car has become like a sanctuary. For me, it's not just a traveling component. I sit in my car to meditate, sometimes write, sometimes cry, or sometimes, I'm in there having church. Don't let the spirit hit me out there, I be done got out of the car and went into praise and worship. Or I will get out and do a dance. Why should I be ashamed? The world doesn't have a problem with worshipping who they are following. Then there are times I just get inside the car, right outside my house just to get some peace. No, the bathroom does not work in my house; my children will come find me. If they have something to tell me, it doesn't matter where I am. Well, while sitting there quiet, many thoughts of tests, trials, and disappointments started bombarding me, probably to torment my mind. I got things coming at me left and right that I have no idea what I'm going to do about. Then it was as if I heard a voice say, "Why don't you just quit, throw in the towel, give up. You're not even accomplishing anything." Those that know me, whether young or old, are forever telling me that I'm crazy or laughing at something I said. I get it all the time. I guess I'm just funny or bipolar. Well, my response to the voice was laughter within, and the next response was "Quit what? I'm not quitting something that I've already won" because my name is VICTORY. I KNOW MY IDENITY. I KNOW WHO I AM!

Does the Enemy Know More about You Than You Know about Yourself?

The other day in one of my writing groups, a friend sent these words: LIVE YOUR LIFE IN SUCH A WAY THAT WHEN YOUR FEET HIT THE FLOOR IN THE MORNING, SATAN SHUDDERS AND SAYS, OH CRAP SHE'S AWAKE.

Well, I loved the passage, and then I thought, hey that must be me. Now I can't speak for anyone besides Lynda Joice, mother of two, wife, baby sister of seven, author, assistant drama director, and the list goes on. I didn't know there was so many gifts inside of me. Yeah, I live with me every day. But I was a stranger to myself. No wonder the enemy been wanting to wipe me out. There are several things he was concerned about, like that I would grow up and become spiritually mature and that I would learn my purpose in life. I don't blame him for being a bit concerned about the person I am. Sometimes, I get a little high strung; I inherited that from my dad, but my dad wasn't one to mess with either. During his homegoing service, folks were saying if you didn't want to hear the truth, don't ask Deacon Taylor. That was the truth. The more they talked about my dad, the more I was like wow, that sounds like me! Still now, after I calm down from being Miss Excitable, girlfriend knows how to war in the spirit. I know who I am and what weapons I have. Nobody is talking about living on a bed of ease. I could be wrong, but I don't believe there is such a thing in this life as a bed of ease. In this world, we all have battles to fight. I have struggled to get everything I have, and even once I get it, I have to fight to keep it. So, I am not too familiar with anything being easy. The enemy has used so many tactics on me, should I be concerned about what his next trick will be? I don't know, but as long as I am in my right mind, and as long as I got something to say, my praises will continue to go before my Savior. There is no time for being laid back and just taking hits from the enemy of this world. I got stuff to do. I have accomplishments to make. I have people to fight for in the spirit. I'm excited about what God is speaking into my spirit. I am ready to use what God has placed in me to give God glory. That is why that old snake was afraid that one day I would find out what material was placed inside of me to support other individuals. That old snake was worried that I would overcome the spirit of depression, loneliness, low self-esteem, suicidal thoughts, and walk in victory.

I Just Had a Thought

Hopefully, this one won't cause me to get beat up somewhere. Everyone is coming out of the closet. So, I guess I can come out with my comment. Here I go with my big mouth, always got something to say. I have always been a bit outspoken growing up. I've gotten better since I've been spiritually mature. I'm not trying to be judgmental nor do I want to offend anyone with the subject. I know we're living in the last days. In the scriptures, it talks about men will be lovers of themselves. That is not excluding talking about women loving other women and yearning for them. Well, I saw a photo of a pretty woman and this other woman looking and dressed like a man. Yeah, I am sure they were lovers, just too up close and personal.

There was no question, just take my word for it. Then I had a thought. I believe lesbians don't trust men or so many men have hurt them they become connected to someone like themselves. I don't believe it is love. I believe they have a need to fulfill their flesh. If lesbians think it is so okay for two women to be in love with each other, then why is one of them always dressed up or dressed down trying to look rough and dress like a man? Huh, huh, huh? They don't want a man, so why they trying to look like a man? Then you got two women both trying to look like a man or two women both in wedding gowns And why are they purchasing a penis to have sex with? Confusion. I have had friends that were gay who were very good friends of mine. I just didn't agree with their choice. What is unfortunate is that none of them will accept that this lifestyle is unhealthy on some many levels. Time for me to go; I have said enough."

Stop Allowing People to Put You in the Trash

Folks look on the outside of us but never know if we are fighting personal demons within ourselves. No, I am not talking about being possessed by demons. I am basically talking about hurt or pain from our pasts that follow us through life. And sometimes still trying to crunch the very life out of us. But we all have a choice of whether we are gonna step up to the plate and live or we could lay down and die. This is how I get through so many things. I speak the word of the Lord into the atmosphere. I will bless the Lord at all times, and His praises shall continually be in my mouth. I believe in giving God the glory that He deserves. Ha, God is so amazing to me. God has anointed me in spite of the things I am facing inside and outside of this body. I had a horrible morning. It just seemed like the enemy was trying to ride my back. So many things that I wanted to accomplish today, just wasn't working out right, and I was ready to say "the heck" with trying. You ain't getting anywhere anyway. Just quit! But instead, I began feeling a bit of fire burning inside of me. I started singing praise songs. I knew I had to get up and get ready for my spiritual mother's Homegoing service. I didn't want to go. I kept hearing her voice in my spirit "just stop it!" something she would often say to me when I felt defeated and wanted to quit. During her service, someone sang, "I Won't Complain." I just cried, repenting for my complaining earlier and then saying "Thank you, Lord" for His mercy once again. Sitting in my old church listening to songs I heard growing up, reminded me about the seeds God has placed in me. I told my son earlier with all I had dealt with this morning; "I guess this is what favor on my life looks like."

We all have to know WHO we are and WHOM'S we are. Especially when we are faced with adversity, struggles, and storms. They have been coming at me one after another. I get up to only be slapped back down. When the service was over, my mother was repeating the family joke about me being the youngest and that my being born was an accident. With her having a 13-year-old child, my mother wasn't hardly thinking about having another baby. Too bad, here comes Lynda. I stopped the conversation and said, "I am not an accident. You may not have planned for me to be here, but I was very much a part of God's plan." That was the first time I had rebuked my mother about teasing me about my birth. She had to laugh at my response. She included, "I must agree, Lynda, you're right."

So, I will say it again: STOP ALLOWING PEOPLE TO PUT YOU IN THE TRASH BECAUSE WE ARE HIS TREASURES AND HE TRULY LOVES US!

CHAPTER 18

I had been trying throughout my life to choose what profession to embrace. In 2009, the Lord began showing me how to channel had been trying throughout my life to choose what profession to embrace. In 2009, the Lord began showing me how to channel all of my gifts, talents, and interests under one umbrella. The recent experiences that had knocked on my door have been mind boggling. And I was beginning to feel a huge shift that was about to take place in my life. Before leaving the church where my family worshipped, I finally was able to go to AIM, Auxiliaries in Ministry for the first time. This is an annual youth conference held by Church of God in Christ denomination. I was excited to be going. I was packing clothes and getting ready by washing clothes. Accidentally, I dropped the liquid detergent bottle down the steps, not realizing that liquid spilled on the bottom step. And down I went. I was so hurt that I could not get up. The only person home was my husband who was deaf. Not to mention I was all the way down in the basement calling for help. I couldn't even crawl across the floor because I was in so much pain. I just laid on the floor. I was taken to the hospital. I ended up having to go on the trip with a brace on my ankle and needed crutches after being diagnosed with a bad sprain ankle.

You would think that would had been enough. We had been in Florida for a few days. I was enjoying being there. I had finally gotten away on a trip. This was like a vacation for me. During the trip, we had a rainy day. I caught a cab to the convention center from our hotel to attend some of the youth workshops. My walking had improved. I decided not to take my crutches. They only slowed me down. The marble floors had no rugs on them. Why Lord? Why me? Why was I the only one to fall? I HAD JUST FALLEN A FEW DAYS AGO DOWN THE STEPS. I laid in the Florida Convention Center in so much pain, crying. I was in shock. I couldn't believe I had fallen again! It appeared to be an unbelievable nightmare. I thought, *Why is God always allowing something bad to happen to me?* I was in so much pain. Again! I was in too much pain to care about being embarrassed. I just wanted to lay on the floor and not be touched. Security asked me if I was alone. My daughter was found. Security had to get me off the floor, but the way my leg was twisted, I didn't want anyone moving or touching me. I could barely get in the wheelchair because of the way my leg was positioned. I had no choice but to go to ER. I told my daughter to go back to class. I didn't want her to miss her workshop. She told me she wasn't leaving me. I wondered if I was going to die from all this pain. I just wanted everything to stop and come to an end.

That fall basically ended the trip for me, but I wouldn't allow my daughter to miss out, so I made sure she continued to have fun while I spent most of the rest of the trip in bed until it was time to go home. I was given an immobilizer that fitted from my thigh down to my ankle at the hospital. That would need to stay on for the duration of the summer. But I sure bought me these gorgeous red shoes. I vowed one day I would be able to wear them. I was unable to do anything all summer besides sit around. Wherever I sat, I could not bend my leg, which meant I had to ride in the back seat of the car with my leg elevated.

All summer I had time to think about what I heard the Lord say to me in Florida. It's time. How was I going to step down from all the ministries I was involved in? I clearly heard the Lord tell me it was time for me to leave my church of over 25 plus years? For quite some time, I had been seeking God about leaving. My heart wanted to be somewhere else. I wanted more of God. I felt like a fish out of water there at church.

I knew my decision to leave was final. I wrote four letters: (1) to the pastor, (2) to his wife, (3) to the minister of music, and (4) to the youth choir director I was assisting. There was too much going on that I no longer wanted to be a part of. I'd been involved with church and choirs almost all my life, and I wanted to spiritually grow.

I had to step away from those that wanted to keep me bound and to keep me in a strange place where I could not grow. God had the final say. He said go because He was in need of a willing vessel.

After leaving the old worship center, our new worship place used initials to identify their ministry. It was a long time before I could even get the letters in the right place, or I was leaving letters out. My plan was to just go visit my son's church in December of 2009, or so I thought. I had been there to visit before, but God set me up. When the pastor's wife gave the invitation to join, I was clueless of what God had in store. Without any notice, it appeared like the Holy Ghost lifted me up and I had glided to the front of the church. I was scared to death. Everyone was shocked. They had no idea that I was just as astonished as they were. I wanted to run back to my seat, but I couldn't move.

My six-foot two-inch son shared through his wet emotions that he was happy about having his family join with him. When the pastor saw that I had joined, he stared with his mouth dropped open.

I fell in love with my new church, my pastor, his wife, and my new church family. This young man is an amazing preacher and teacher.

Services were inspiring and uplifting. I looked forward to being there every time the doors opened. Both of my children also loved to attend. It was especially a blessing to be in a small family church again after being in such a large congregation. I just kept thinking that this church was unusual and too good to be true.

All I wanted to do was learn more of God, worship, praise the Lord, and go home. I believed that the word was being taught there, and that was the main factor for me. I had decided that I was not joining anything. I just wanted to sit and listen to the word be taught. I didn't want to meet any of the members neither. I didn't want new friends, and I didn't want to talk to people. I was fine by myself. I didn't want to ever get close to anyone else in life again. My plan was to keep my distance. Yep, a wall had formed around my heart, and I didn't really want any other person changing up on me.

Welp, all of my plans were thrown out the window. I had not been a member long when one of the young women became drawn to me. I don't really know how it happened, and it took me by surprise. I remember her telling my son, "Your mom is my mom now, and there is nothing you can do about it." My son was like, "Oh, alrighty then." That kind of thing happened often with me and young people.

I didn't become active in church until about a year later. And that was not something I had volunteered to do. I was appointed over the Fine Arts Department. That decision was a total shocker to me, especially when my spiritual daughter allowed it to slip from her mouth, thinking that I already knew. And when she said it, I thought she was joking. I don't know why the pastor thought I was qualified for the position, but I began creating programs and different events almost immediately. I later created an event called the Youth Explosion, which I have continued having yearly. The theme of the first youth explosion was "You are a star." It was very much like a talent show. Then other events were birthed, especially with the youth in mind. We even began having skating parties, too.

Maybe about a year or two later, I was appointed vice president of the Mother's Board, which I didn't want to be a part of at all. Here they go again putting me on something I didn't agree to. How did I get nominated and placed into this position when I wasn't even present for the meeting? I tried to get out of that position more than once or twice. Mother's Boards are for women who are older than me even though I did have the capability to teach, lead, and help assistant younger woman. I already did that automatically. But being on the Mother's Board just felt weird.

This new worship experience felt like I had been born again. I wanted to rededicate my life to Christ.

Our pastor preached regularly out of town, and he took his congregation with him. I wasn't sure if he understood how much we loved and believed in him and his ministry because supporting him was easy. Unfortunately, a shift began to take place. I began having dreams that I tried to ignore, hoping they were not true. What I began doing more of was praying about the things God was revealing to me.

No one could have convinced me that I would grow to be so unhappy at the church we grew to love. Too many people were hurting, and there was inappropriate sexual activity going on among the leaders with church members. I could not sit in the midst of the continual disrespect toward the older church members. Some were being spoken to in disrespectful ways by leadership. I was hearing from God about leaders being dishonest. God was showing me how much the ministry was out of the will of God. I was hearing God speak to me during service, and he was showing me things in my dreams. I didn't say anything being others did not appear to notice. Plus, I had not been a member as long as some of the others were. I was asking God questions. Why would He allow us to be in a place where we loved to serve Him and the ministry be snatched away?

Lord, help me forgive that my family's church was stolen from us.

Sometimes, a person is given gifts, and then the person becomes haughty and full of pride. There is nothing or no one that is to come before God, not even a ministry. The Lord reminded me of the story of Nebuchadnezzar and how everything was about him; he wanted his way at any cost. Nebuchadnezzar was a king that controlled every aspect of people's lives. They had to bow down to him; otherwise, he had them killed. Not to mention, this king was an example of Lucifer—look how fast he got thrown out of Heaven for being haughty.

Not Many Listened to Noah Either

There were several times way back in the day that many people were given a word to share to their families, friends, and other people. Folks did not believe those news barriers either. Even when the people spoke or gave visual signs, the people did not listen nor did they believe people like Edison, Ben Franklin, Einstein, Harriet Tubman, Dr. Martin Luther King Jr., the Prophets of the Bible, Noah, and Jesus Christ. Choose this day whom you will follow and whom you are going to serve. Whether we make a conscious decision or not, we all are serving someone or something. We bow down to this, or we either worship something else. I don't care if a person is an atheist or not, everyone bows to something. An atheist may not worship God, but she or her believes that God exist—why would they hate something that they believe doesn't exist? Denying things does not make something not real. That is just your opinion. People also don't believe global warming is happening. Either you believe it exists or you don't. Time will tell of its truth. We watch many movies like *Twister, The Day after Tomorrow* (one of my favorite movies), *War of the Worlds,* and *The Day the Earth Stood Still.* We watch the effects on the world on the screen and say that was a great movie or not such a good one. Never once do we believe these things can happen to our world. Movies tell a story either bad or good, real or not real. Okay, what about Hurricane Rita or Katrina? Were they movies? Folks, wake up! God is speaking through the weather and also in the movies. "Oh, God didn't write the movie, some person wrote it." Can you prove that God did not inspire the writers to write? No, you cannot, and I don't have to prove anything either. Some of us are living in cities that are about to be destroyed forever. Don't keep thinking the Bible is just some history book, telling fantasy stories that are obsolete and or will never happen. It is five in the morning now, and this is what was laid on my heart to share. We all can close our eyes to the happenings in our world. And we can continue to keep on sleeping and not believing that destruction for some is on the way. Look at the economy, guess that is a dream, too. Yes, some things do happen because of our decisions and because of the choices we have made. But nothing can or will happen that God does not allow. He is in control regardless of how it appears that He is not in control. And best believe, He will take care of His children. He always does. Even after death, His children will be fine because there is the possibility of a better life on the other side of living here when our journey here is over. There are people I don't know and love living in some of these cities that one day will be destroyed. Many are entertainers and celebs. I don't care how much you got or how much you think you got it going on. We all are going to die one day, and I am praying that folks get out of those cities safely. But in the meantime, I am praying before death or destruction comes to them that individuals take out a LIFE POLICY with Jesus. No one has to believe me. Not many listened to Noah either. But the handwriting is on the wall.

The Special Gift

We all have been given the gift of life. The air we breathe is only on loan to us. At any time, the lender can draw His air back. We also have been offered the gift of Jesus Christ so that we can live life and live it more abundantly. Sin separated us from God. Because God gives us free will to. But Jesus came to carry us back to the Father. We have the opportunity to receive the gift of the Holy Ghost to give us direction, to teach and guide us into all truth. Everything that we learn throughout life is not all truth. We learn and hear many lies that lead us to physical, spiritual, and mental death. Last but not least, many of us were given the gift of a loving mother. Your mother nurtured and wiped your tears away whenever you fell or was hurt. She encouraged you when no one else cared or understood. She loved you beyond your faults and mistakes, and kept you close when others threw you away. Your loving mother continued to pray and pray and pray for your healing, deliverance, your life, and your soul.

A loving mother, God's gift sent from Heaven, picked from His garden, designed especially for you.

And for those who may not have a loving mother, I apologize. But God always makes up for the shortage. God gave us the gift of Jesus Christ who will love you just as much and more as a loving mother. Lean and go to Him. Jesus will understand you just like a loving mother, and He will embrace you better than any mother. And just like a momma, JESUS will always love you and never throw you away.

Call on him for everything and for anything. He wants you and waits for everyone to spend time with Him.

CHAPTER 19

Even with the twists, turns, ups, and downs that come from looking back over experiences and encounters, my life amazes even me. I've been diagnosed with diseases and ailments that reacted differently in my body than others. One disease I was diagnosed with that society evaluates as incurable is basically inactive in my body. A woman with a phenomenal anointing over her life said to me that she saw the disease in my body dry up. God designed that miracle especially for me. Various medical issues continued to pop up inside of and on me. Things continue to keep trying to claim my sanity and my life. And God just continues to cancel them all out. No one has to tell me that I am a survivor, a survivor who speaks out loudly every time I wake up in the morning. I am a survivor on active duty.

For a certain amount of years, I carried a dark mark on my right bicep about the size of a quarter. It didn't bother me, nor did it hurt. But it could not be bumped nor touched by anyone. If that did happen, it was an everlasting rippling throb. It still continued to get darker and darker. My doctor had a biopsy taken of it which came back negative of cancer. Praise God! But it still needed to be removed. After the surgery was over, my daughter told me that the tumor was the size of a baseball, which was the reason it began being visible. The tumor was larger on the inside than what it appeared on the outside. It had grown out of room inside of my arm. The first time my pastor saw the scar after it had healed, he mentioned to his wife that he thought I was involved with a sorority or I had been branded. Many strangers see the scar and think it's a tat, but it isn't. It's a scar left behind from 83 stitches. My scar is often a conversational piece, giving me the opportunity to tell people how God was so merciful to me once again. There had been the possibility of me losing my arm, which meant I would not have been able to write stories, plays, or journal. How devastating that would be to a published author and playwright. God just continues to heal me over and over again. How can someone overcome so much and not look like the things they've been through. Being a praying woman, no doubt, has gotten me through so many practical and spiritual challenges.

It took some time, but I finally came to the conclusion that it was ok being me. I didn't have to be like others, including those who shared my bloodline. I'm not meant to be average. I tried to slip into a glove that didn't fit me. For years, it was uncomfortable to be different and set apart. My son said, "Mom, you're not the ordinary 50-year-old. You're unique." Obviously, my son's comment was correct. I ran into a woman at our old church, whom I hadn't seen for years; she told me that she was about to give up on life because she had just turned 50. But now that she had seen me, she admitted that I had encouraged her that she did have a lot to live for at the age of 50. She said, "You look great."

We never know who we encourage just by waking up each morning and being the best we can be. I learned to be comfortable with being the person God created me to be. I have always done things completely different than everyone in my family. I learned there is a reason why I was born to be peculiar. I no longer stay inside of a box that was not meant for me to be in the first place. People were trying to put me there and keep me there. But when I began to act out this revelation, I felt a release. With that discovery, I had a huge coming out birthday celebration at a hall. That was an evening I will never forget. So many people attended. We danced, had a lot of food, played games, and laughed a lot. That's my kind of celebration.

There are many healthy and safe ways to express and act out your feelings. We all need a way to release anything foul growing inside. Too many folks are holding on to struggles that are weighing them down. In order to be completely whole, you must stop being too busy not to treat and take care of yourself. Love on yourself so that you may live an abundant life. Find your happy place. Being prideful can be deadly.

CHAPTER 20

I remember it being said that I was the lady who goes around talking about "stop bullying." It started with having a youth event named "Youth Explosion." It is a talent show that spotlights youth throughout the city that rap, sing, dance, perform spoken word, etc. Some performers even came from out of town. I had speakers come in talking against bullying. I experienced being bullied, so becoming an advocate grew close to my heart as an educator. Then, I went in deeper after hearing how many youths were suffering, hurting, humiliated, and committing suicide.

We always say how sad something is, but then we do nothing. There have been too many senseless deaths because of hate crimes. There are too many individuals in our society who enjoy watching people hurt. I wrote a skit titled "Just Imagine" about a boy who bullies students on the street while he is being bullied by his mother at home. She is an alcoholic who uses her son for sexual pleasures. This boy has reasons to be angry. My intention is to create this skit into a longer production. I wrote it because who thinks of helping the bully? Me. To get rid of any problem, I believe what is needed is to get to the source, to get to the root of the problem. Oftentimes, the bully is dealing with demons of his own, including those that he may live with inside of his home that cause isolation, neglect, and anger. This bully may be living in an abusive, drug-riddled, or alcoholic environment. Who knows, they even may be victim of a sexual abuse. There is a reason why a bully takes advantage of others. My desire is to create a youth anti-bullying program. I desire to use theater as a platform to give youth that have been affected by bullying to express what they feel. My intention is to allow the youth to help create this bullying program. But have you ever heard, nothing in life is free? Grant money is highly needed for the Vision Productions Inc. Praying that my networking is blessed with the right individuals to assist. Too much money is being wasted on the wrong things in this world. I will not give up. I believe there will be opening doors of finances and favor for new youth programs, for new youth opportunities, and for new youth events.

So many times, I wrote blogs to help get me through some tough days. Below are some of those posts.

You Keep On Looking Out for Me

I don't know how many times I have heard
Kirk Franklin's song, "You Keep On Looking
Out for Me." It is part of my playlist in my
office. But for some reason today, I heard the
song in a different light. I don't know what it is
about my car. But it seems to be my spiritual
sanctuary where the spirit of the Lord dwells
and speaks to me.

These words made me reflect on some
experiences. "In spite of all I've done, you keep
looking out for me." In my spirit, I felt, "In spite
of what I go through, you keep on looking out
for me."

All the many hurts, disappointments, and
attacks on my mind and on my body. "I know,
Lord. "You keep on looking out for me." I
don't understand a lot of why some things are
going on in my life, but, Lord, "you keep on
looking out for me."

In the Bible, the enemy pulled all types of
attacks out on Job. His marriage was
challenged. He lost all of his children, and he
lost all of his wealth. And most of his health
was hit and challenged to almost death. He felt
alone and desolate. But "God kept on looking
out for him."

Joseph in the Bible, who I often say is my
twin, was the youngest offspring, and he was
also a dreamer. His own siblings were
intimidated by him, and they got rid of him by

selling him. He ended up in slavery and was lied on by this floozy just because he wouldn't give her any booty. Though Joseph may have had a little chip on his shoulder, and he maybe was a little spoiled, he still didn't deserve none of the treatment that he received from others. But because he was anointed, he had to face many challenges that could have broken him emotionally and mentally. Instead, however, Joseph grew wiser and ended up being a great blessing to many generations in his family because God "kept on looking out for him."

So, what are you saying, Lynda Joice?

Don't turn down a true foundation in Jesus Christ. Things do get tough at times, and they often may look hopeless and dim. But Jesus is still on the throne, and He is still God! He will "keep looking out for His own." And He will keep those in perfect peace whose minds stay on Him. You ain't got to be alone. God is available. He's able. And He is our Advocate. Lean and depend on God. You too will also find that "He will keep looking out for you, too."

Look Here & Hear

See, it is because I know who holds my future that I am motivated to keep moving forward. Now, I am not going to lie and say everything is always a bed of roses for me. But I must say when things don't look great, I know where to go to regroup. Yes, there is some pain, sometimes more than I would like to think about. But I have a choice whether to accept defeat or pull myself out of a state of mental defeat. I also must say because of the many battles that there must be great blessings that will be birthed from inside of me. See, a lot of why life gets so crazy for us is because we are on the right road and because we have a banging future ahead for us. We have huge battles in our lives because there is something we must learn. Or it is to teach us how to wait, how to depend, and how to trust our God. Patience is a virtue, but not too many of us have it. Sometimes, we must learn more about who we are and about the gifts and talents that God has placed inside of us that we didn't know we had in the first place. We have to see more on the spiritual side of life and not always see the natural side that causes us to be deceived and upset. Donald Lawrence sings about "The Righteous Mind" and "Let the Word Do the Work." Seek God's Word, learn it, and speak it into the atmosphere. We have a mouth where curses or blesses can be used for our benefit. There are times we have to mature and to be strengthened in different areas of our lives. Truth be told, there are times when we may think so much of ourselves that we are no earthly good to God, and He needs to bring us down a notch before He can use us for His glory not our glory.

My daughter inspired me to write this nugget because, Lord Jesus, thinking about her journey got me so excited. For the past several months, I have seen that girl in action. Yes, she had some highs and some lows, but she went after what she needed accomplished. I've seen her buckle down and sink her teeth in a goal. I saw her frustrations when she was about ready to give up. Nope, that was not allowed on my watch. There were roadblocks of people telling her what she could not do or could not have. And she was like whatever, you must don't know who my God is and who I am. She had praisers, a cheering team, and prayer warriors that were on duty. The girl was on a roller coaster ride since August of 2012, physically and emotionally. When she hit a roadblock, she either ran through it or went another way. She even slowed down sometimes, but she eventually got more gas from her talks with God. See the enemy knows my daughter has an exceptional love for babies and children. She has a plan and goals that will blow up the enemy's kingdom. And yes, my daughter won the battle, and she will continue being a Conqueror through Christ Jesus our Lord. Dr. Sanders is going to be awesome. She continues to prove that. "Look at Me, I Am Changing" must have been her theme song.

We all must have the type of determination my daughter had in order to accomplish the goals that we have. We all must grow. So many of our goals involve other individuals. Our lives are not for us only. We each are needed in the land. We are the light of this world. Our lights cannot be hidden. We all must shine. Our lights come from the love of God that was placed inside of us. There are people who need to be told that there is a loving God that wants to commune with them. He is a God that wants them to come out of darkness into His marvelous light. People are dying right before our very eyes without knowing the love of God. They don't know that God is a healer of sickness and diseases. They don't know that God heals the broken hearted or has so many blessings for them that they may not have enough room to receive. They don't know that they can have the type of freedom that Kierra Sheard sings about in her song, "Free." We can't give up. We got to have determination. If you run into a roadblock, let the GPS reroute the direction you are going and keep your destination moving forward but in a different way.

God wants us to be who He has created us to be. After all, He gave us tools to use for a reason. Get from behind that 8-ball and SOAR!

Don't Have the Sarah Spirit!

Without faith, it is impossible to please God. This is what God's word tells us. The Lord wants us to love Him. But He also wants us to trust Him. It is an insult when we doubt what God tells us. Sarah was old; her husband was old. But they were given a promise from God that Sarah would give birth to a son in her old age from her own womb, not from the womb of her servant. Sarah laughed when she heard the news that she was going to be pregnant, then she denied that she had laughed. She laughed because 'she didn't believed she could still have a baby since she was past the age of childbearing. Is there anything too hard for God? No. Little becomes huge and impossible when you put it into the Master's hands. God is not like man, so He cannot lie. If He says He's going to do something in our lives, we are not to doubt His word. None of us like to wear that coat "WAIT." And because Sarah felt she needed to help God along the way, because she knew she was too old to have a baby. Sarah had "her man" sleep with another woman. Foolishness! And that lunacy is some of the reason why there is a mess going on today in the Middle East. Wrong choices do affect other people, and the effect of the choice may never go away. Just because something God promised us is taking a long time to manifest does not mean that God has changed His mind. We are not too old to give birth to seeds that God has planted inside of us. Maybe we have not dilated enough yet. Or that baby you are carrying may just not be quite developed to come forth yet. But God says what He means. Just because we think it's time, does not mean that God agrees. So, while we are waiting, we are to be seeking Him and working while it is still day. Let us not get weary while waiting for the manifestation because the promise of God is we will reap what we sow as long as we faint not. Don't give up. Don't abort that dream. Yes, we want something from God, but God also wants something from us, too. He wants us to trust Him and have faith in Him, no matter how long it takes. Continue to trust Him. He is an on-time God. Yes, He is! Don't laugh at God like Sarah did. Don't take on Sarah's spirit of Doubt.

CHAPTER 21

Anytime I stay away from church for over a year, something heavy has occurred. I would keep praying and seeking God for direction. I questioned whether to leave my present church or to stay. Things just were so messy there that it was interfering with my focus on serving God. For two years, I was not a member of a church. My emotions were unsettled. I was very saddened that something so unexpected had happened in a church that I adored. It was like a grieving period was going on after losing a loved one. After a few weeks of not attending my church, I wrote my letter of resignation and left as quietly as I came. Learning church etiquette growing up, I understood that there had to be closure. Also, under the circumstances, I knew that it was best for my dignity and spirituality to move on I could not stay in a church where leadership told untruths.

The church nightmare thrusted me into not having a home worship center for over two years. That had never happened to me in the 50 plus years I had been alive. I had dealt with things going on in church all my life, and I put up with the nonsense of the people I had to deal with in church. But I didn't want to deal with church nor church folks anymore. One thing I must say, I did learn some things about myself through that separation. My daughter and I, after a long period of time, began visiting a well-known church that I had always wanted to visit, but I could never visit because I was never available. I would usually be too busy in my own church of worship. That was no longer the case. I loved the spiritual experience, the word, and the choir, and the praise dancers during the services, but there was no doubt this church would not be where God would plant me.

A few months after my son had joined a new church, my daughter and I went to visit. I had visited there once before but declared that I wouldn't go back. The church was just too far.

The day that I went back to visit, my daughter had discovered a quicker route to the church. Sometimes, the things this young woman knew amazed me. The route she drove took half of the time the way I had driven before with other people.

The sermon spoke about a family's past church situation and their experience in their church. And there the Lord goes talking to the matriarch of my family in service, me. I mean God was really speaking to me while the pastor was preaching. And yes, I had questions I was asking God while I listened to this profound sermon.

So much happened in that Sunday morning service in September. I heard, "Follow your son. Join." And I debated with God: "But, Lord, I can't, this church is too far to travel." I paused. I kept telling God why I couldn't join there. God told me to trust Him.

The pastor opened the doors of the church. I sat and refused to get up. As the pastor was doing the call to discipleship, four people came to the altar. And silence was golden. The pastor said, "There is another, and we will wait." No one moved. Then I heard these words, "What if you don't live another day? Tomorrow is not promised." I sighed, then I slowly got up on my feet. Church was so quiet that if a pin dropped it could be heard. I wasn't happy about taking this walk with all these perfect strangers' eyes on me. I was shaking as I walked down the aisle, knowing everyone was watching me. It appeared to be the longest walk in history. I didn't remember ever feeling this terrified before. I stood at the altar, feeling nervous. What the pastor said next appeared to be prophetic. He said, "There is one more, and she's a young lady." No one moved. I began wondering if the pastor was referring to my daughter. I began praying "Come on, baby," and whispering my daughter's name in prayer.

The vision of seeing my daughter come down the aisle with her brother was like a gift to a mother from heaven. The pastor addressed my daughter as she came down speaking in her heavenly language. "Keep speaking, baby." The Holy Ghost had a great grip on my daughter's tongue from the whole time she left her seat. I was amazed that we had joined.

The services were good. What I enjoyed the most about being a member of this church was the fellowship that my family had after service with a few of the young people. As usual, I was well known to having young people around me. Even though I am very leery about allowing myself to get close to anyone and I usually don't talk much to anyone I don't know, for some reason, I grew to love each one of these young people at our new church. After service, we would go out to dinner and just laugh and enjoy each other's company. I never wanted to leave them. I didn't want to go home.

During this time, I would be numb for hours from the pain inside and the heartbreak and disappointments that I was dealing with in and outside of me. I was considering going to counseling to channel my thoughts, but questioned if that was the best thing that I should do. I had so much going on in my head.

A few months after we had joined, one of the connections opened up a doorway in which I allowed a young lady to live with us. She was close to our family and also a member of the new church we had recently joined. I was told she didn't have a place to stay and only would be with us for a few months. I never thought, *Why can't she go stay with her parents?* But I was glad to help. I just could not imagine her living on the streets. Not to mention, we really trusted her.

From what I saw, my family made adjustments, and the young lady was comfortable living in our home. I heard no complaints. It appeared to be fun and enjoyable to have an addition to our family. But things don't always appear what they seem until you get up close and personal.

Some months later, things started coming out of the woodworks unannounced. The young lady was telling lies to her family members and other people about us. Then after dropping these nice nuggets, she would act innocent and confused that she didn't know what others were referring to. She became very disrespectful toward us and our home. Later, when things began to hit the fan, two of her people confronted me and my family. I found out that she had told others our personal business. I was called names. A family member told me that they were going to tell the pastor on me. Tell the pastor what? That we allowed your family member to live with us? What else are you going to say, that your family member was living rent free in our house considering she did not work? I am not sure why some people think they have so much entitlement and authority. But none of that threatening fazed me. Why was I concerned about her telling the pastor as if that was going to scare me? It didn't. My daughter concluded that she felt I was being taken advantage of. So, my daughter kindly asked the young lady to leave. But this young lady wasn't making any arrangements to leave. She had become very rude, causing confusion and refusing to leave. So, I had to begin packing her things. A few months had turned into over a year. Things got so off balanced that things almost turned physical. No one comes in my house, walking around, acting like people are invisible, living free in my house because you angry. It is time for you to go. I believe that no one has the right to come into anyone's home and cause havoc. Yes, I got angry because here you are in my house causing discord. She was telling her family that I said things against her character. She was lying and making up other lies to tell other people. Just lying for no reason. No one bothered to ask our side of what happened. They took her word against mine. She lied for no reason.

That experience taught me a lesson. No matter who they are or how much they need help, it's better to help someone find help somewhere else outside of living in your home. I decided after some time to just let all of those involved with the whole situation go. They were individuals I had to learn to forgive for the lies and disturbances. Holding onto grudges only blocks the blessings that our Father wants to give us.

After about two years of being a member, I didn't gel well. I realized there was just too much pomp and circumstance going on there. People were more into putting on a show to be seen because the pastor was a famous celebrity. So many people came to show off their church outfits. Most of their services was about music and shouting. Not too much time was spent on helping individuals with their spiritual walk. Not a lot of focus was on prayer or bible teaching. I had never been a member where the pastor was gone almost every Sunday. The pastor was always traveling. He was always MIA. And if I wanted to focus on all that singing and playing music like they did in church, then I would go to a musical concert.

I needed to be in a church that was more spiritual. For me, there was not enough time spent in prayer or worship. I had missed singing on the choir, so I joined. I felt that going back to singing was what I needed to do, but that didn't last long. It wasn't fruitful singing the same songs over and over. It was mentioned about me directing the choir, but I said no thank you. I didn't feel led to direct. Things just appeared to be messy.

Too much was going on in my personal life to have to be somewhere that created more misery instead of a place that fed the spirit. Here I was being challenged at home, in my finances, at my job, in my health, and in my marriage. Our utilities in the house were getting shut off often. I was bothered that our house needed repairs that we could not afford. Something was always breaking down. It appeared that I was carrying so much by myself like most of the time. During winter months, we would be cold. We would apply for programs but get turned down being told we made too much money. You have got to be kidding me. My job didn't pay for holidays, they didn't pay for snow days, and God forbid if they paid us during the summer. For the summer, I had to find my own employment. That is how I ended up driving for Uber and Lyft. You can't tell the bill collector, well, I am a 10-month employee, but for two months, I have no income. They don't want to hear that. THEY DON'T CARE! So, I would fall behind on my bills every summer. I would never get caught up because my place of employment would not pay the paraprofessionals a suitable income. I was drowning. And I was fighting depression. For whatever reason, depression thought it was my best friend. It would leave for a period of time, then come back with vengeance. My health was somewhat of a challenge because of diabetes, stress, and carrying other people's burdens. It wouldn't be the first time either that I had questioned whether or not I was losing my mind. Why wasn't I praying? I was praying a whole lot. My journals exemplified that I prayed often for others, friends, family, coworkers, my church, my birth and spiritual children, even strangers that I met. But it seemed like I didn't pray enough for myself. Only thing I can think of as to why I didn't pray for myself too much is that the less I thought about all of the negative things that were going on in life, the better I was able to help myself get through the pain.

As awful as this sounds, I was also experiencing some months passing clots of blood from my body. They would be so big I could feel them passing through me. But my most major concern was people seeing this red evidence on my clothing. I did the best I could to keep this a secret, especially when I was in church. Who wants to deal with that embarrassment? Individuals always ready to talk behind someone's back whether it's fact or fiction. Society would be surprised about the many women living with fibroid tumors— modern day women "with the issue of blood." Church is a place where healing is to take place.

One day, something hit me about our place of worship that really bothered me. This church did not have regular communion. They only had it once a year. Did this church understand what communion represented in the life of a Christian/believer? My family went to churches that were accustomed to serving regular communion, focus on prayer and bible study. We were used to corporate prayer, where members had the freedom to pray, walk the floor, kneel, or lay prostrate, setting the atmosphere. This is what we longed for. There was no bible study classes where the members could ask questions to the one teaching the class. Church is supposed to have the focus on worshipping God. By the words that were frequently repeated, the church was more into worshipping the pastor than worshipping God. They were coming across like a dictatorship and a cult. I felt like I was at a circus being entertained.

More than anything, this church believed in shouting for almost everything. From the pulpit, people would be instructed to begin dancing to provoke blessings from God. I believe the pivotal mission is about soul winning and life changing. God wants relationships with mankind. If individuals come not knowing the purpose of what church is supposed to be about, then shouldn't there be leaders who teach what Jesus did and what He wants.

Judgment is not intended toward the church. That is God's job. I heard the Lord speak to me during a service that I would be leaving soon. For weeks, I was feeling rather uncomfortable. So much going on was vexing my spirit. It was as if someone were scratching their nails on a chalkboard every time I attended. Not long after praying for direction, God suddenly stopped me from attending. This was the first time I ever left a church after being a member for less than two years.

I have been asking God a question for some time now. And on Monday, March 30, 2015, God gave me an answer to my prayer. It was an answer which I wasn't too sure that I liked. But I'm glad for the fellowship with my Heavenly Father because in His answer there was clarity.

My question was, why did I have to deal with the types of experiences that I had in my life. What was I supposed to be learning? And though I believed that we go through experiences not necessarily for ourselves only. I wanted to know what were the purposes of these experiences that knocked at my door.

How many times do we say "Lord, use me for your glory?" How many times does God choose to use us in a manner that is uncomfortable or use us in a manner that the experience may make us unhappy? And sometimes, it can be an experience that is long, and God may not move quickly. Then the next thing we say is "God, never mind, I don't like this. This is getting on my nerves." Or, "This is too hard."

I've said "Use me, Lord" more than once or twice in my lifetime. Since my youth I've been active in church ministry.

So, God gave me an answer that what I am living is a form of a sacrifice. Not that I am anything like the magnitude of Jesus Christ. No way am I equal to Christ in no way. But God reminded me of how He used His only son to be a sacrifice for the sins of the world.

So, the Lord told me that day that a portion of my life was like a sacrifice for many others. Your sacrifice will speak life to someone. Your sacrifice will teach someone. Your sacrifice will help give someone a ticket to peace of mind. I choose you to go through this because you will still continue to trust me. You will still continue to praise and worship me. Someone needs to see you holding on and going through their valley so that they will learn and know how to go through their valley by watching you. When it gets really tough and tears fall, you still know how to hold onto the horns of the altar. This is why you have your father's praying mantel on you. I once was blind, but now I saw the truth.

God needs us to be witnesses for others here on earth. And through tough times, we cannot waiver. So, yes, my answer from God on Monday, March 30, 2015, was you were chosen for this sacrifice to prove that you are an example of an overcomer of life. You are a conqueror over anything with the Lord's help. When others see your success journey, they will know that they can be and do anything through Christ Jesus. It can be done through prayer. Speak affirmations about who you are becoming with confidence. Don't lean on your own understanding and always acknowledge

Him in all that you do. Stand flat footed and protest Jesus never forsakes and that Jesus will never leave you. Protest that Jesus never fails. I am a living testimony. Yes, life can be hard, but you can still win. Fight for your victory!

CHAPTER 22

For the first time in my life, I decided to enroll into a mentoring class. The course description was to *bring wholeness, team building and to discover our gifts.* The class was divided into three parts: "intimacy with God," "discovering self," and "birthing your purpose." We did a bit of note taking, and our mentor also gave us writing assignments. The thing I didn't like was her strongly persuading us to talk in front of her and our classmates. Ugh! I hated that. But because I wanted results, I complied with everything I was asked to do.

In the very beginning, the question we all were asked, *What was your childhood like using two words.* I got annoyed. My two words were "unhappy" and "suicidal."

Our mentor was always making us discuss topics that were taboo to me. Like, I didn't want to discuss about my childhood, no more than I wanted to discuss about my marriage. Each one of us was given a one-on-one appointment with the mentor in which she had us discuss those taboo subjects that I mentioned. And I was always caught off guard by her tapping in where she knew exactly the right words to reach into my soul. In my session with her, she asked why I was always hiding. She had compared me to a turtle that began to stick my head out and run back in. That was a portion of my homework assignment—to figure out why I was hiding. I discovered why I was hiding; I realized that I didn't want anyone looking at me. Those eyes that leered at me as a child, that sneaky smirking my way, those words of me being pretty—all by the man who molested me—that was why I didn't want anyone looking at me. I was uncomfortable with receiving compliments and receiving attention. My answer to my mentor's question was packaged into going back to when I was molested. My mentor also encouraged me to smile more. "You have such a beautiful smile that lights up a room." That was not the first time I'd been encouraged to smile more often and that I had gorgeous bedroom eyes. I believe I was afraid to smile because I was frightened what my smile would promote or provoke. If I smiled, I could give off the wrong impression. Would I be sexually violated, again?

When it came to discussing my marriage, I considered it off the table, but my mentor was insistent. I didn't want anyone encouraging me to stay. Unless someone lived in our house, an individual would never understand. I had sacrificed a great portion of my life to a marriage that gave me very little in return. It was so empty and unfulfilling. I just wanted to be happy with a good measure of peace. I didn't want to hear no scriptures thrown at me either. My thought was, *Yeah, 'til death do we part, but what type of death do you mean? A physical death, an emotional death, or a spiritual death?* That is what I heard in my conversation with the Father. And we all know you can't withdrawal nothing out of a bank if there were no deposits. Or if you don't water a flower, it will die. And inside, things had died inside of me. This was my personal thought, *"You can't expect to receive anything from anyone if they do not have what you need from them. Moving forward." Marriage was not to be one-sided. It is a partnership where individuals have to share themselves to the person that they vowed to be with and not be self-centered. And after more than thirty years, I was exhausted with trying to feed a dead horse. I wanted the conversation over. I didn't want to have to prove why I had the right to be happy. I just wanted her to mind her business. She had not walked in my shoes.*

CHAPTER 23

For several years, I was going back and forth fighting to keep the home we lived in for over ten years. Because of the loss of two incomes, our finances had depleted. As a family, we felt scared and discouraged about the unknown. This battle was unlike any fight that I had ever encounter. We kept receiving encouraging words from our supporters. I had friends that were praying and believing God with us, but this trial was monstrous. We continually kept receiving threatening notices from the mortgage company, from the bank, from lawyers, even from the sheriff's office informing us that we were going to lose our home. Our backs were definitely against the wall. We felt trapped. Debts were breathing down our necks. We were out of funds. We didn't know where we would live. We were afraid that we would end up living on the street. I kept thinking how did we get in this mess. None of us had been homeless before. Yes, I blamed myself on numerous circumstances. Had I done something wrong? I refused to tell my family for fear they would ridicule me or our dilemma. I could hear words of judgmental accusations that we should have done better with our finances. Some didn't really understand the issues that occurred where I was employed. Then on top of that, medical challenges with my husband's health were brutal. He wasn't about to look for a job. We hadn't signed up for any of this combat. But it was real, for real. This was not a reality show.

Doors weren't opening no matter which program we applied for. No matter the program, I kept being told we didn't qualify. We were scheduled for court date after court date. I had to keep taking off from work. I possibly faced being terminated from my job if I kept missing time from work. I couldn't believe we would end up homeless. We were quickly running out of time. The threatening notices to evacuate came religiously. Many nights, my sleep was interrupted. I was stressing. We all were searching through newspaper ads, rental engines, and even seeking by word of mouth. We had ventured out to see a few houses. But even that always led to a dead end. Individuals were promising to assist, but no matter what we tried, everything fell through. I had been afraid of things before in my life, but this creature from the black lagoon had me terrified.

I was numb. In a month's time, we lost our house. Someone asked if I was embarrassed about losing our home. No, I wasn't embarrassed. We weren't the first individuals who had lost their house. Regardless of the years of financial investments that we had poured into that brick structure, we had to move. We lost the fight. It was scary not knowing where we were going to go. I was shocked that we had lost the fight.

Packing was an ordeal of its own. My God today and tomorrow. Where did all this stuff come from? I realized that I owned items from each of my talents and gifts. But owning all of this stuff was plain ridiculous.

About thirty days before we had to move, we were told by a relative that there was a house available on the west side of town. That was at least 45 minutes away from everything and everyone we knew. It would take me almost an hour to get to work. Then it would take longer than that if there was traffic. It was in a community where I didn't know anyone. I would have to Google and GPS everything to get familiar with the area. My children and I had never lived in no other area in Philadelphia. For those reasons, I could not accept the house especially being so far away from my job. So, I told the person no thank you and we would keep looking. While continuing our search, I heard in my spirit, "Why are you limiting me? Why are you keeping me in a box? Stop worrying about that job." All I kept thinking about was how God told the Bible character Abraham to take his family and go to a strange land that was unfamiliar. Once we decided to look at the house, we were told another family also wanted it. Too bad, did that family belong to the Lord like we did? I remember me saying to the landlord that I wanted to have a word of prayer. He was an Israelite, so he agreed. We took each other's hands and approached the throne of grace. Well, the other family didn't get the house. We did. A couple weeks before Christmas, with the help of some friends, coworkers, and family members, we moved into the house in the middle of a snowstorm. Happy holidays!

In all the days of my life, I never expected that I would ever live in West Philly. Living in that area really felt as though I was in a strange land. This really was a leap of faith.

After moving so far away from what I knew, day after day after day, I wore a permanent isolated suit. Several times, I had to quiet my words and thoughts. I was not happy where we had moved to. It felt heavy. There was always trash on the street or pathway. I hardly ever walked on the sidewalk. Sometimes, even a dead mouse would be outside. I am petrified of any rodent, dead or alive. The block was tight and only had parking on one side of the street. Parking was also scarce. I never had that problem on the old block. These folks didn't appear to leave the house. It didn't matter what time of the day; they didn't appear to move their cars. Trying to get a parking spot was horrible. One night, I almost spent the night in my car because there was no place to park. I could not leave my car parked where it could be towed. That neighborhood clearly was not very safe.

Philadelphia is an old city and possibly the whole city had old gas pipes, especially West Philadelphia. There had been three gas leaks on our street in the one year we had lived here. The first gas leak was early in the morning; the gas company came banging on doors, trying to locate the leak. It was across the street from our house. The third time, gas seeped into our house from outside. We didn't smell it, and it could have taken us out during our sleep. My daughter had moved out into her own apartment. So now it was just the three of us. Right before the gas company came banging on our door about 8:30 a.m., my son had just left for work. Using their special instrument, the reading determined that we had to evacuate immediately. It was another miracle for our family that. Had we been stirred to an area that really was not safe. I didn't know what we could do about our living arrangements. My family didn't really know where we lived. I didn't want them to know. And I really didn't feel I could talk to any of them. I felt I needed time to be alone without the judgmental comments, the control and the opinionated remarks. I only wanted positive people around me. People that believed in change and that actively prayed, not just talk about that prayer works. You cannot pull me out of the gutter if you are in the same level of gutter with me. I had so many negative thoughts about our move, and I had to silence my words and thoughts, which led to a whole monologue to myself:

At least we are not living on the street. Remember, y'all were close to being homeless. Remember how petrified you were? Now you got good heat. Don't you remember how cold that house was? You had to figure out every winter month how much oil to buy for the winter. You finally have a shower that works. Which is major for you. Girl, you love showers. Lynda, you have always wanted wooden floors. Now you have beautiful wooden floors. No carpets. You get to go in a home that has a new kitchen and new bathroom. Silence the lamb. Just quiet yourself. Regardless of how the neighbors perform, you get to go inside, close your front door, and mosey on to your awesome bedroom and king-sized bed. Those belong to you. Girl, this too shall past. God has always covered you. That will never change. Trust the process, be patient, and be quiet. You have no right to complain about anything.

On top of that, I couldn't figure out why I was so angry and impatient. I was in labor with my body and more changes in my life. I felt different. I looked different. And truth be told, I was different in so many ways. I'd been in so much pain emotionally. Just hurting to the point that I couldn't verbalize. I would break out crying. I would have anxiety attacks. That was something I wasn't accustomed to experiencing. Anxiety attacks were triggered because of so many changes happening in my life all at once.

Whether these changes made sense or not, they were happening while I was giving birth to a new future. I had been evolving. Unknowingly to me, I believe my transformation began in my spirit first, then in my mind and then certain transformations were bursting on the outside. I remember being told often that I looked younger and that I was glowing. But I didn't think much about their words to me. There were times I had mood swings. I was feeling weird on the inside. I didn't want to be around or talk to a lot of people. I knew I had been placed on a different plateau. Things had shifted in my life, that I felt I did not owe anyone any explanation. God had changed me, and everyone had to accept that.

One evening after parking my car around the corner from my house, I walked down our narrow street and was taken back to my childhood. This street was so similar to when I used to live near railroad tracks at the end of our block. We lived on that street until I was about 9 years old. It came to me that I had been sent on this new narrow street to start my life new and fresh. This was the way to go back to my childhood. God wanted the little girl Lynda to be healed of all that childhood brokenness so that I could be made whole. I heard; trust the process even if it may not make sense to how you feel or what you see. Know that there is greatness in you that has to come. God told me he was going to show me how to use all of my struggles to help others.

Some may look at your smile and hear your laughter but never know the darkness you could be carrying inside. In many instances, I had outlets to link to like preparations and rehearsals for the production of "Are There Virgins." One day, I drove around the arts area downtown desiring to put on a new production. That same day, God heard my prayer, and I received a call from my nephew who was also a minister. He wanted to do a collaboration with me. I was interested being he was connected to a few organizations. What really blew me away was when I found out that my brother's son was pastoring the church across from the School of the Arts and Kimmel Center downtown in Philadelphia. Whaaat!? I was in the lap of the community I wanted to be in.

Shift is what I learned to do. You just can't stop moving in the middle. Keep going! Things were unfolding, and I was excited about what I had envisioned.

CHAPTER 24

The year 2018 appeared to be the year of personal losses. It reminded me of 2002 when we lost my dad and other loved ones all in one year. Now a bunch of losses in this one year was the real culprit that had me thirsting for a therapist. I had lost three people within weeks of each other, all of them close to my heart. Things and people were suddenly drifting away, either by death or physical separation before my very eyes. "God, grant me the ability and courage to accept things I cannot change." I was generally closer to males my age instead of women. It had even been that way growing up. For years, my best friend was a male until I got married.

My close friend, who became my brother passed in October. I was devastated. I became the assistant director of his production company in 2003. He was a minister with a phenomenal way of teaching the word of the Lord. He had been one of the ones to speak a word over my life. Working with him inspired me and gave me the courage to branch out with my own production company, the "Vision." He battled with his health periodically for years. He had been in a coma and survived. A couple of years later, I believed a blood clot took him out of here. The list continues.

In my birthday month, I lost another loved one, my spiritual mother who died from having four strokes. Two of the strokes she had at one time. The other strokes followed later. I believe she also had a broken heart over her youngest son who died a little less than a year before she had her first two strokes. We became confidants quickly in 2009 and grew amazingly close. She and I spoke like every week, sometimes two or three times a week. She didn't have any daughters, only two sons. I was the only daughter that she ever had. What was crazy? When she had her first two strokes, her job called me. She had slipped into unconsciousness and could not speak. They called me. I was the first number that showed up in her phone being I was the last person she had spoken. My God, she was creative. She made clothes and was an amazing cook. Not to mention she had the gift for interior decorating. She could dress and wear a mean hat with shoes to accommodate her ensemble.

In the same month of November, a few days before my birthday, my spiritual sister who knew me since my teen years passed. Her family had brought her back to the city where she could get the medical care she needed. She could no longer live down south. Her cancerous brain tumor had returned so violently. The last conversation we had before she slipped into a coma, she quoted so much of my childhood back to me. I was in awe that she had remembered a lot that went on so many years ago. She remembered my secrets as a troubled young person and talked about me being suicidal and depressed. But she wanted to remind me of how anointed, gifted, and musically inclined I was in music, directing, and writing since I was a teenager. She told me that was why the enemy had always been on my back trying to ride me and trying to destroy me since back then. That he knew the impact I had on other people. But he wanted me dead. She was telling me how proud she was that I never gave up and kept moving forward. This pulled on my emotions because she had paid that much attention to listen to me as a teenager enough to recite that to me as an adult. Someone did really listen to me as a child. Someone really heard me. My big sis told me she was bragging on me and going around showing people down south the different playbills from the productions I had written. She made people believe that I was famous. Her advice to me was to study Psalms 23, "The Lord is my shepherd." But she blew my mind when she stated, "You think God is not gonna to honor the sacrifices that You always made for your husband while he was sick. And for taking care of your children by yourself still during those times? She said to me, "I know you wanted to walk away, but you stayed." Just hold on. 'Cause, baby, God's coming to bless you." These are words she told me before she left this Earth. I hadn't seen her in over fifteen years. But we reconnected before she died. I didn't know she was as sick as she was. When I visited her in the hospital, she told her nurses about me directing the choir and that I was a producer of my own productions. Even in her weak days, she prayed for me and spoke life into me and my situations. She knew me so well. She understood me better than many others did. She knew me better than most. And I believe God was using her to speak to me and to prepare me for what I had to endure with what was coming up next.

In January 2018, this was another loss. Though this was a physical loss to my body. I had a laparoscopic abdominal procedure. My uterus had dropped so low that my cervix was protruding outside of my body. This procedure left me empty inside. I was not only losing people. I no longer had a womb. They crushed her up and removed my girl from inside of me. I was extremely nervous about having the surgery. I was concerned about being in pain afterwards. After surgery, my family was told there had been complications. What was supposed to have been a three-hour procedure ended up four hours. I remember coming out of recovery feeling giddy and happy. I was on cloud 10 and a half. Thank God there was little to no pain during my six-week recovery period. My body had conquered my major fear, and for my recovery, I had to focus on allowing my body to heal. During that time, God was working on me through my conversations with Him. Ninety percent of my healing included forgiving others completely. There were things in my mind that were clogging where I was destined to go. Forgiveness was more for me than for whoever offended me. I had to let every negative comment, every negative person and every negative thing GO!

Some individuals determine that women are no longer women after they have had a hysterectomy. That is a lie from the pit of hell. I was incredibly happy that the procedure was performed. No biggie, I was fifty-eight years old. I no longer had to worry about an unwanted visitor each month, and I didn't have to worry about no babies. Free sex, ha! The losses in my life didn't stop here.

I was preparing to leave my job, but I had not planned it this way. Six months after surgery, my retirement from the school board became official. I couldn't believe I fell outside the school building on the concrete steps on the way in from lunch. When I fell on the job, I was injured. My employer did very little to compensate me. I ended up walking with a cane. I would be in excruciating hip and back pain. I also injured my wrist from falling on it. The sciatic and herniation that I faced daily was new for me. The sciatic nerve in my back was causing pain to radiate down my leg, affecting my walking. As a Lyft driver, sitting for long periods of time only agitated the nerves and limbs in my body. Medication and physical therapy were what the doctor ordered. But do you know when God steps in to take care of His children, He does all things well. What man meant for evil, God turned around for my good. Leaving that place was a dream come true. It was a release of unspeakable joy and peace inside. I would finally have the free time I desired to work on my goals, work on my heart's desires, work on my purpose in life, and gain my solitude. That place was draining me, taking advantage of me, and did not understand my worth in this Earth. I had bigger fish to fry.

What seemed to happen for bad actually was turning around for my good. Being separated away from everyone and being in a strange community did hurt, but it was for my good. I needed to grow and be allowed to be the person that I was meant to be without opinionated and unwanted comments. It was not meant for everyone to understand the changes in me and in my life. Not everyone understood who I really was anyway. Trying to make me fit into others' frame of being was stifling and suffocating me. That had to stop. I was never meant to fit into anyone's ordinary box. I was not ordinary. Being different was my destiny. There were too many around me that were incapable of embracing my uniqueness. Too many individuals close to me could not handle that I was different and that I was unique. That is why I was thrust way on the other side of the city. If I had not lost my house, I'd still be stuck into being someone that I was not. There was a butterfly that was preparing to spread her wings.

It appeared I was becoming another Lynda. The real Lynda. The free Lynda. I looked and felt different. My thought pattern was not the norm. I felt somewhat weird, but there was a peace that was engulfed inside. This process was taking me through a period of metamorphosis.

The other conclusion I came to—I had to get Lynda Taylor back. She got lost. I'm not sure how losing myself happened. Where did Lynda go? This was where the psychotherapy came into place. I wasn't crazy, but I needed assistance to get untangled and needed help clarifying some things. I needed to get out of other people's control.

I signed up with a mental/behavioral health specialist. I wanted help organizing my thoughts to keep my head from popping off. So much was going on all at once, trying to take me under. But over the years, there was a fight inside of me where I learned never to quit. I wanted a professional to help me put pieces into perspective without being judged. Isn't it comical that I didn't want a Christian therapist either, being all deep and over the top? I didn't need anyone on my team being extra for no reason. But I did want someone who would take me seriously, listen, and not think I was loco. I had therapy before, and I wasn't ashamed to go back. Most of the individuals around me didn't even know I was going just my adult children and two of my girlfriends.

To me, this was my plan for self-love. I no longer cared what others thought about what I did or did not do. I didn't need anyone to tell me what to do or what not to do. I wasn't suicidal. I had no thoughts about killing myself. Plus, I no longer wanted to drive off of a bridge. Just the opposite; I was ready to live. And I wanted to live it up to the fullest. I wanted help to make sense of this chaos that was going on in Lynda Joice's head so that I could move forward. I was really ready to be happy and retrieve the joy, happiness, and peace that had been stolen from me when I was young. I wanted to make peace with my childhood, my past, and with those I felt had damaged me. There were repeated tapes and images that I wanted to let go of forever. Do not come back tomorrow. I was ready to write everyone an eviction notice. I had to learn not to live in my head so often. Too much was riding my emotions. If I had to let go of people or things, then God had provided his signature as approval. It was time to set goals and achieve those goals. Life would move on without me if I didn't let dead things go. I remember being told that I was the slay Queen. Now, Queen, let's slay whatever is needed. It was time to cut the dragon's head off.

I was on the road to not just detox physically but detox emotionally, mentally, and yes, even spiritually. This girl was on fire. I'm going to get the baby healed that wasn't wanted. I'm going to give the teenager the love that is embedded inside. I'm going to acknowledge the confidence that the woman sweated for. It was time for this woman to SOAR.

I began affirming more and more my self-worth. I would repeat affirmations out of my mouth. I had enough of the disappointments, nonsense, and any dead weight in life. I had too many challenges coming at me. Yet, I knew that I was created for bigger and better. I still love God, and I am still a part of the body of Christ. I just no longer desired to be a member of any church organization. I feel that I have been detoxing from old church principles that hindered true fellowship with God. My time in prayer was revealing to me that so many man-made principles had nothing to do with salvation. God wants our heart. I always wondered why certain rules and regulations going on in some churches used to bother me. The fact that I was no longer a member of a church was quite a shocker to some people who have known me for years. I don't expect most to understand. With this transition in my life, I spiritually just needed more of God, one-on-one. I may assist in a church service if I am led to. But I am not being led to membership.

I am so geared toward reaching out beyond the four walls of a church building. I was given a gift to love people even when they didn't show love back. It had been placed inside of me how to love people from their hurt place. The revelation that was given to me was some individuals didn't have it in them to return love because they were broken. Too many hearts, minds, and emotions need healing. How many of us acknowledge this without inflicting a person more? I used to want to be a therapist. And I remember one of my girlfriend's mom suggested that I not take on that task. She felt with the type of compassion that I had that I would get too close and become too involved with my clients' problems. She ain't never lied. I often feel that protecting others from any type of foul behavior is my responsibility.

If churches are going to collect all this money in offerings, then they need to help feed the homeless, build housing, clothe the naked folk (even though some like being naked). Help people receive medication and help them get off of drugs. Help people pay for medical and life insurance. Help this dying world, physically, emotionally, and mentally like Jesus said and did. I've heard people say that spiritual gifts are not for church. I believe spiritual gifts are for wherever people are whether they are in church, on the street, in the market, in a salon, in school, on a job, or even while driving for Lyft. Spiritual gifts were not given to prostitute.

On December 31, 2018, I finalized the decision that I wanted a whole new life in me, around me, and on me. I yearned to have so much of me be made new. I didn't want to drag anything old into the new year. Changing my hair color wasn't something new. I have been dark blue, light blue, blonde, two different types of pink, mixed bronze, copper, and emerald green. But praying, asking the Lord what color should we change the color to was new. I asked the Lord what color should I change my hair for my new me. I believe I heard the color purple. Wow, never thought of purple hair before. Okay, let's go for it. I was bold and daring. This possibly could be the last color for the rest of my life. I am going to be an angel walking around heaven with purple hair. I already knew purple meant royalty. Later, I Googled the color; it also means creativity, wealthy, spiritualism, mysterious, and magical. Anyone that knows me knows that every one of those meanings fits me like a glove.

My desire for change is manifesting in so many areas in my life. I am learning how to move past those things that have disappointed me. I am healing from rejection and from other defenses done to me. I didn't realize I was feeling abandoned. It was time for me to heal for real and completely. Burn up all negativity for my New Year for my new life. I pulled away from all people and things that wore any negativity on them. I decreed and declared to learn to be patient and not be so sensitive. (I despise that thing.) Kick out rejection, kick out feeling insecure, kick out worry, kick out low self-esteem, and kick out doubt—all of them, forever. Be positive. Believe in me. Be confident. Know that I am victorious. Smile more and aim high. Be kind to myself. Love Lynda first. Go back to dreaming again, dream big. Rest more. Smile more and learn to mind my business. Some individuals I cannot help. Unfortunately, the truth is some don't deserve me no matter how much I want to help them. Lynda, some people do not deserve the awesome gem that you are. Give them to the Lord. Pray and intercede especially for those who weigh heavily on your heart. I needed to take my life back, to make affirmations over me.

Remember to speak life over yourself and over your life. WATCH YOUR TONGUE! Watch and control your thoughts. Stop overthinking situations that take you into a dark place. Lynda, look up and live. God is your Father, and Jesus is your best friend. Show love to yourself all the time. Remember, always be pleasant and SMILE often. Do not be in such a hurry. Pray, meditate, and talk to God just like He is your Buddy.

Make exercising a main focus in your weekly routine. Stay motivated. Put a huge smile on your face no matter what. Treat yourself often. Get facials regularly. ENJOY LIFE! Laugh often, laugh a lot. FORGIVE OFTEN! Have fun. You have always enjoyed music. Continue to dance when and wherever you desire. Who cares if people are looking? I will break out in the market dancing in a minute. Who cares what people think? Remember to eat smart. You only have this life to enjoy. Learn to relax as much as possible. There are more things to learn in this world. Study, research, read, write often. CREATE. SAVE and be a good steward over your money. Work on becoming debt-free. Wealth come to me! Continue to make wise decisions. Discover new things. Begin to embrace an abundant way of living!

My name is Lynda Joice. My name means beautiful/joy. Lynda means beautiful. Joy means a feeling of great pleasure, and I make goals to be HAPPY. Joy belongs to me; after all, joy is a huge portion of my name.

CHAPTER 25

It was time to *taste the rainbow*. New Beginnings. New Day. New Season! New Health. New Strength. New Body. New Way to Rest. New Thoughts. New Thought Pattern. New Mindset. New Insight. New Connections. New Goals. New Way of Living. New Outlets. New Ways to use some of the old outlets. New Relationship with my Father-God/Lord and Savior. New Faith! NEW! NEW! NEW!

Metamorphosis

Breaking things down to crush old pieces was a must. I got rid of things in my house, including getting rid of all black clothes. I didn't want anything dark and black around me. I only kept a couple of black outfits for when I had to sing. I got rid of all my red clothes, which was once my favorite color. Somehow, I grew tired of red. I didn't want to own anything red anymore. I was becoming new inside. I was transforming. I also had my piano removed out of my house. It was old and out of tune. I just wanted as much newness around me as possible.

I believe this transition started happening before the manifestation began coming forth. I knew I felt things change inside of me. Yet since I had been dealing with so many things all at once, the change appeared to come suddenly. Like BAM!

The Professionals

In order for me to completely overcome my past, I needed to be resuscitated. I had to embrace all over again the things I loved to do. I had to get clarity about every aspect of my childhood, my birth, my teenage years, my relationships with my parents, my siblings, my family, my adult life as a woman and as a wife and as a mother, etc. I had to connect the dots. I had to learn Lynda. Who was I? Learning myself consisted of me asking some raw questions about myself. I had to face my truth.

To assist in that process, I found a professional therapist. In my sessions, there came times I had to admit the ugliness and ugly experiences that didn't feel good. I had to dig deeper than ever before. I had to touch on things that had been hidden and tucked away inside my heart and in my emotions. There were many things that had to be laid out on the table. Time to kill the negativity planted inside me. I had to get at the roots. It was time to kill believing that I was just a pawn in someone's game. Time to kill letting people around me act like they didn't have imperfections of their own but always pointing their fingers at me. Time to prioritize my life. I wore baggage that was unfairly thrown on me. Baggage that had become unfavorable weights. Ugly baggage that was not meant for me to carry.

Shift, Lynda is what I kept telling myself. You deserve to be happy. Shake those grave clothes off. Time to come out of that cocoon. You want more in life, and you deserve better than what you have been given. You were created to be a butterfly with wings to fly. It's time for your season. It's time to shine like a diamond. Shift your mind, shift your thoughts, and change your verbiage to positive affirmations. For some time, I had been speaking affirmations. I watched individuals on YouTube talk about affirmations and the mind. I was listening to them repeatedly. Then, my mouth would go right back and cancel them out. But that had come to an end. I was learning to shift my words and my thoughts. Think big and set big goals. Lynda, follow your dreams. Life is made to live and to enjoy. You are living under an open Heaven, believe in even the impossible. Trust the God that created you. I was learning to shift and focus on what my mind was shifting on.

Letting go of bitterness and disappointments was slowly working. I was in the process of not allowing images and past conversations run like movies in technicolor and perform inside my mind. These affected my emotions. Killing a toxic mentality was a major goal for my wellbeing. I had to face it, speak it, and cut certain stumbling blockers from working actively in my life. I was finally healing for real. When people came speaking garbage to me, I denounced their lies. Some, I had to denounce their whole presence from me. It didn't matter who the person was. Them and their negativity had to be released from around me. Some folks we just have to love from a distance. Some folks will never change, and that can clog the flow of our happiness, joy, and peace. My accomplishments were productive, and it felt wonderful.

I knew it was so essential for my well-being to have discussions with my clinical professional. There was too much ricocheting, bouncing, and colliding in my mind that felt unhealthy. Honesty was the best policy. I knew I had to have someone I felt comfortable with so that I could be totally transparent. I couldn't accomplish a thing with someone being judgmental. Otherwise, I would only be fooling myself that I would conquer any deficiency if I didn't tackle the broken pieces of my soul. I needed more than just to exist. My goal was to survive and be whole.

My sessions compiled of topics covering my marital relationship, my children, my extended family, and my interaction with others in my life. We talked about my goals that I wanted to accomplish. We discussed how was I coping with moving into a community where I was a stranger. We discussed those changes in my life as far as no longer wanting to be married, leaving my job, and leaving church attendance. I was fed up with just about everything. I was no longer tolerating certain types of behavior. I was a different individual in so many ways. And the facts were I had a great portion of my support team. I was disconnected from church membership, disconnected from my family, disconnected from my job, disconnected from my female organs and disconnected from husband. I was disconnected from a lot of things that I no longer had interests in. I grew to knowing that I deserved a better, peaceful life. Even the health changes in my body caused by diabetes, pain, physically falling, and no longer having the female organs that carried hormones, eggs, or children were real. I occasionally had mood swings and unwanted thoughts. But truth be told, I was beginning to finally feel happier. There were even times when my therapist and I laughed and talked about how wrong the meteorologists were about predicting snow that didn't fall.

The professional diagnosis: mild depression. And I knew how to fight for myself. Fighting was embedded in me from my childhood. And since I had been down that road before of saving Lynda, it was time for the last round, and I was gonna kill this demon for good with an assistant. I am a confident conqueror.

I was faithful to the weekly treatment plan. My new confidence fit me like a glove. Those irritating loose puzzle pieces that were jumbled up in my head were connecting. The great thing that I appreciated most was my therapist acted like a down to earth human being. The missing pieces that I had been dealing with he knew how to help bring clarity for me. Plus, I was grateful that our sessions were interactive.

My therapist was a great listener, but he also shared some things about himself. He was from North Jersey. He told me about his parents, his family, and we talked about his professional career and his hobbies. We talked about his education and his past growing up with a sister that was much older than him. Just like me. I also found out that his wife was expecting a baby very soon. They already had a son but was excited about their new addition on the way. I later found out that my therapist grew up in Church of God in Christ faith. I found this funny because I didn't want a Christian therapist. But he stopped attending church when he was 19. He said he preferred resting and being with his family on Sundays. Once he got older and his children were grown, he said he might consider going back to attending church services again. So, he had grown up in church, but he did not use any religious components in his practice.

My new therapist was always interested in any event that I was a part of. Usually, he would start our sessions inquiring about my weekend. He was such an encourager. If I had to reschedule or inform him that I was running late, I had his personal cell to contact him.

In March of 2019, I mentioned to my clinical therapist that I had met a personal breathing/meditation strategist that could help me go deeper in helping myself. This expert specialized in stress management. I had met her at a workshop for youth and adults given by an associate of mine in regard to mental health. I became interested in the services she offered that had helped others with physical and mental healing. I listened to others give their personal testimonies that she had worked with. I wanted everything damaging, negative, hurtful out of my body, out of my emotions, and out of my mind, too. My plan was also to get off of medications. Why not give some new opportunities in my life a chance?

By the feedback that my clinical therapist gave, I detected he wasn't too keen on me adding someone else to my healing process. I believe my therapist was concerned that an added professional would interfere with my progress and threaten the work we had accomplished. Maybe my therapist felt I would slip back into the old world that I had left behind. It didn't matter to me what concerned my therapist. This was my life, and my decision was to propel forward. I made my choice no matter what he thought. I wanted all monkeys off my back.

Strategist/Breathing Coach

After the breathing strategist's presentation, I asked to speak with her privately in May. That's when I really felt drawn in. I was intrigued by her knowledge and wisdom. It was as if she were able to see inside my soul. She discussed that a weight was placed on our lineage through our ancestors as they endured slavery. This rather educated woman schooled me that quite a bit of our defeated mentality came from slavery. The slavery mentality was passed down from generation to generation.

Generational curses are forms of bondage passed down throughout a family. What she informed me was our physical freedom was not the only thing stolen from our culture during slavery; so many other assets were also stolen. Furthermore, on top of this great heaviness of brokenness, we were never taught how to release these wounds that were injected into our DNA. That statement blew my mind, and I never forgot it. So many generations were struggling with things passed to us and then passed down to our children and children's children that were affecting different areas of our lives. Some of us learned to deal with wearing issues that were beat into us that we were not supposed to own. My God today!

I was amazed when the breathing strategist told me that the first day she met me that my presence was powerful. I was told that there was an amazing aura on me that changed the atmosphere when I entered the room. It's funny that I have been called an atmosphere changer many times before. We discussed the possibility of us meeting again to discuss my needs further.

Unbeknownst to either of us, my medical insurance from my employer would be shut down after I had fallen on the job. Without medical insurance, it turned out that I could no longer be treated by the clinical therapist. Therefore, meeting this strategist breathing and meditation coach came right on time. Who would've known? God knew. God, my Provider, was still taking care of me and still placing strategies in order for me. God had already put a deliverance stamp on for my complete healing. There was nothing going to stop what belonged to me. It was my year. It was time to burn up all substance and take out the trash. It was my birthright to be complete, be confident, be free, and be whole. I was already experiencing and seeing circumstances turning around for me. I was practicing what I learned daily on the three calls I had every week with my new meditation strategist coach. I had email recordings and notes that I logged in my breathing/meditation/affirmation book. No matter what, I was intentionally smiling more. Not smiling too much had become habitual from my cavalier attitude. But I had changed that negative practice. After all, I really do have a gorgeous smile. I now smile even in my house when I am alone. My strategist coach would often say, "Smile, bring up your countenance." Smiling more is really helping to change my life, even my inner-self. Smiling more is giving me such a great charge. It was time to do the work with my new group.

Our group sessions on Tuesday and Thursday morning during the week were 30 minutes. The Sunday evening group sessions lasted about an hour. Our personal coach taught on topics about rejection, breathing, meditation, anxiety triggers, confidence, etc. She gave us recipes that were effective solutions. One of the holistic techniques I loved the most was taking spiritual baths. This detailed getting in the tub and touching your body while speaking positive affirmations over yourself. Declare and decree a thing and so it will be established. I often communicated with our personal coach through text, emails, and maybe once in a while a phone call. As little as these techniques might appear, my life was improving. Control over my emotions was improving. I was affirming while getting dressed, during the day and sometimes I listened to recordings going to bed and to sleep. I repeated and listened in my car. I had recordings on my cell. I was excited how I was even succeeding at becoming more patient. That was an attribute that I was affirming into my life because I had learnt that being impatient was a culprit to many of my challenges. For one thing, I was receiving more clarity to who I was. My mindset and language were taking on a new face. I was learning how to let go, move on and most of all not feel so much of the residue of weights that had latched onto me. I felt my healing taking place. It was amazing. I often used these learnt techniques when I felt bothered, impatient, annoyed, or if my emotion shifted into a dark place. Glory to God. It was working for me in an amazing, incredible life changing plateau.

What was quite surprising is that my life coach was a license unchurched evangelist. No matter what, unchurched or not, she had a strong belief and faith in God. It was so refreshing for her to acknowledge the prophetic, spiritual, and practical person that I was. She was also a believer that believed in being unchurched like I did. Truth be told, I enjoyed being unchurched, but there appeared to be a war going on inside being that I grew up in church. I was not in a backsliding state. I was more than just a Christian. I was still saved. I still loved God. I was getting to know Him even more on a personal relationship. What had become more important to me was having a one-on-one relationship with the Lord. She understood that. There was no judgment. She shared with me her practice of fasting and consecration. Finally, I had someone who still loved the Lord and understood that I was fed up with the foolery going on in so many churches.

My circle of relationships and connections had changed. Should I say my circle was expanding? What I loved most about this newness was these individuals branched from various walks of life. My big sis' words spoken in 2018 to me that God was going to honor my sacrifices was manifesting, and I was tremendously excited about what was beginning to take place in my life.

My life is positively unfolding slowly. But it is a beautiful process. Sometimes, the ride is rocky, but this transition is tremendously appreciative, effective, therapeutic, and healthy.

Thoughts of negativity and worrying about others was no longer on the forefront of my days. That was subsiding. I did as much self-talking to myself that was needed. My wellbeing was on the top of my list. Time to love Lynda first. How can anyone give to others without giving to themselves? Focusing on using all the gifts and talents within me to brighten my day became my focal point. It's so rewarding and joyful to use everything positive inside of one's self. Then watching the manifestation take root. Self-talks bring so much enrichment to life. These outlets that I enjoyed helped me not focus on physical pain nor on the disappointments that I had encountered. Shift your thoughts, Lynda, affirm what you want, breathe, and meditate. Smile, lift up your countenance. That smiling became a weapon.

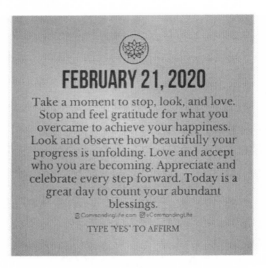

Image from Life/Strategist Breathing Coach

SugarHouse

Being in the SugarHouse Casino in Philadelphia was an experience to remember. My daughter attended with me. The whole purpose of the Women's Conference, "Magnify Your Essence" was epic for me. On

June 30, 2019, I received the "Magnified Mover" Award. I was interviewed by a local radio station. The food and fashion show was tasty to the eyes and taste buds. There was an amazing female photographer there that offered a photo shoot to everyone. She obviously had polished her craft well. Watching other community builders receive acknowledgments was a joy. This shows again that using a person's gifts and talents can be beneficial when used correctly.

Outlets

These are my outlets that have been effective for me.

Everyone's outlets differ. Yet, your outlets are all needed for your survival as an overcomer. Outlets are conditioned to suit and fit the individual. Your outlets are personal. Your outlets can be created from your needs, from your likes, from your desires, from your talents and created from the gifts placed inside of you. Your outlets will bring fulfillment for what you need in your own personal life. Outlets can build a person's self-esteem when used wisely. There's the butcher, the baker. I am the candle maker. A craft of mine is making candles. All of the ones I make are scented and given away. I generally make them as gifts. I enjoy being a creative. Working with my hands has always been an outlet used for healing, but it also is a way to give to and inspire others.

There are various ways my writing outlet has been used to reach out to others of different races, culture, age brackets, and genders. In the past few years, putting my hands to the plow has been evident as a playwright and producer of amazing written projects. Our production company, Vision Productions Inc., is unique being we have the mission to teach, encourage, and inspire. Our latest production "Behind the Keys" is about mental illness which has been performed three times. The third time occurred because it was brought back by popular demand. Each time, the production gets better with more attendees. Each time, we had a full house. The reviews were phenomenal. Each performer delivered performances that drew in the audience through visual storytelling. I love theater. And it is so dynamic to have the gift to write, produce then, watch others bring the written words into fruition. I am praying that God gives me multiple messages to create and bring to audiences.

Another outlet that we have created under Vision Productions Inc. is our Youth Explosion event. This is an event that brings awareness against bullying/cyberbullying. We bring in presenters to speak in regard to their experiences with this growing epidemic. We have had a physical trainer come and teach exercising techniques. Someone comes and does face painting. The day is also laced with performers that sing, rap, perform spoken word, and dance, and vendors who come with products to sell. We learn, encourage, teach, support, network, and have fun all at the same time. I feel led to do something, no matter how small, about putting a dent into this bullying that is attacking the esteem of others. The youth and productions will forever be my brand.

Physical Fitness

It's been about four years since I rejoined the gym. I have physical goals that I am working to meet. I want to lose weight and strengthen my muscles. Not to mention I am fighting against diabetes to get off of this medication. For the first time in my life, I have learnt how to box with boxing gloves. It is good for the cardio and is a good exercise for my arms, shoulders, and my back. I found that sitting in the sauna is good for loosening tight muscles. Diets never worked for me. Changing my eating habits is a challenge. But I won't turn in the towel to defeat.

In saying my affirmations, I have included eating more vegetables, fruit, beans, and protein, and to drink mostly water, sometimes milk. No soda.

Lyft Driver Chronicles

Until January 2020, I was an active Lyft driver for close to four years. Before that, I had been an Uber driver for close to three years. But that didn't end too well. Yet, I enjoyed driving and being a Lyft driver. I have had quite a few memorable experiences that stick out.

Like the husband and wife that I picked up on her birthday. Their family had been out celebrating. They both were drunk. Their son ordered the ride for me to take them to New Jersey around 11 p.m. Once a driver accepts a ride, it can be too late to cancel. The dad was actually the character. He was upset about finding out that his son was gay. He asked if we could make a stop to pick up a sandwich on the way to their Jersey home. I didn't mind but needed him to direct me to the restaurant. I wasn't familiar with the store or the area. The husband got us lost and blamed me. The wife was very pleasant. She and I laughed about marriage. She called her husband an idiot. Every time he cussed, she told him he wasn't being nice and to stop. He agreed. We never made it to the restaurant; he changed his mind because he didn't know where it was. He couldn't even remember the name of the store. Then, sir, I don't know what to tell you. Before I knew it, the husband became disrespectful. He was upset with me because he had gotten us lost. I apologized to the wife because she was nice. But I put them out of my car because

I wasn't taking his drunken nonsense any longer. Sorry, ma'am, but I need you both to get out of my car.

Then there was the time I waited a bit for a young lady. She was placed in my car by someone. I thought the person was getting in as well. But no, only one passenger. She was literally dropped on the car seat. Plopped! Maybe I'm just naive. The girl stretched out on my backseat. I warned her that we were a few blocks away from her destination. No response. When we arrived, I called that chick several times, no response. "OMG, what if this girl is dead." I didn't know what to do. I flagged down a cop by slamming on my breaks. Girl flew off the seat onto the floor. The officer came over with his flashlight. I explained that this girl in my car would not respond after calling her numerous times. He pointed his flashlight in the girl's face. Her falling on the floor woke her up. She was like "What is going on?" It was the officer that reiterated what the problem was. Somehow slamming on breaks, flashlight in the face and seeing the cops sobered her up almost immediately. The officer had me follow him to her destination. When we arrived, she looked out the window and said that was not her house. Mind you we went to the address that was placed in the Lyft application. The officer told her to get out of my car, and she staggered out. As soon as she climbed out, I locked my door. She tried to climb back in my car, but too bad. As soon as she stepped away, Lynda Joice pulled off. Then I pulled over down the street and reported the incident. Lyft reported I did the right thing. Lyft customer service said they always want their drivers to be safe.

Once I got a call that pulled me into a domestic violence situation. I ended up calling 911. I had to leave the girl at the pickup spot because the guy kept slamming my car door shut, not allowing her to leave. I didn't care nothing about him cussing at me. But I was annoyed for the girl, so I called the police and prayed. I would have drove off with her in the car. But she was unable to get in.

Young people rode in my car often. I had a young man get in my car. Told me about his life, how he had lost his grandfather and was raped by some individuals at a group home. There was another time when a young lady got in my car saying she felt God in my car. She started crying and kept on venting to me about her job and how people were taking advantage of her. She said she knew that I was a Christian, she felt the warmth when she got in my car. I prayed for her. I have had people ask me to pray for them in my car. A young man sat in my car crying, his date beside him. She was white, and he was black. He was crying because they had just left a place where he was degraded for being a black male in front of her. She took it lightly that he was made to be embarrassed by cops in front of her. He voiced that cops often harass him because he is a black male in this society. He made it known that she would never understand. That broke his heart because she never supported him. They argued in my car the whole time. When we got to their destination, I asked if I could say something. They welcomed my advice. I just gave them words of encouragement, and I prayed for them. They left smiling and thanked me.

The story that was most devastating was the girl who went off on me by hollering at me. She got upset because I didn't respond to her comment. I thought she was on the phone. She talked to me the whole 45 minutes in the car. She was grieving about being drunk and rolling over on her baby and suffocating the child. She was so drunk that she didn't know what she had done until the next day. When she woke up, the baby was dead. She told me she would never be able to forgive herself for that, especially for drinking. She just wanted to kill herself but knew she couldn't. When I got her to King of Prussia at her job, she asked me if I would come back to get her when her shift was over. She said she liked me because I listened to her.

Lyft had become like a ministry for me. I have experienced numerous different stories and lifestyles. Not to mention God had sent people to uplift me. Like the woman who mirrored so much of my life. She was an older

Christian woman who I was taking to the nail salon because she barely could walk. She told me her pain left by the time she got out of my car. After hearing testimony, she said knew that God had placed her in my car. I knew it, too, when she shared with me that after 30 years, she got a divorce. She told me that the Lord said that He didn't pick that husband for her. That man she married was her choice not God's choice. And that was exactly why things were not going well in her life. My eyeballs almost fell out their sockets when she told me what God said.

Ms. Jackie's story alone wasn't the one that really blew my socks off. This one took the cake. This man I picked up in the middle of the day wanted to direct me to his destination. He was against the GPS. In his opinion, it took drivers around the mulberry bush. This man talked a lot. He kept talking and talking. I was in a hurry to get him out of my car because he was talking so much. But his story became rather interesting, so I listened without interrupting. He was annoyed with God. There were some things that had happened in his life that he felt was God's fault. He talked about his teenage years. Some of his experiences made his heart hard. He didn't trust people. And he definitely didn't want to hear anyone talking about God. The only family member that he was close with was his praying grandmother. She often prayed for him. And prayed he would accept Christ. He wasn't thrilled about her trying to recruit him toward God. But he loved and respected his grandmother, so he didn't verbally refuse her.

During his growing up, he was a troubled young man. He ended up in jail. But when he got out, he got in more trouble. His father told him if he didn't do better, his dad was afraid he would be killed on the street. His behavior caused him to be distant from his parents. The only person he did listen to was his grandmother. So, he enlisted in the military. I was thinking why is this man telling me all of his life story. He just went on and on. He begun not caring about life and ended up homeless. He had slipped into depression. He looked bad, roaming the streets. One day, he roamed into a church. The church folk were afraid and leery of him. He was raving and carrying on in the church. One of the deacons took him in the back and talked with him. He ended up accepting Christ. He came in that church looking for his grandmother. It was his grandmother's church. But that was the Sunday she did not attend. The rider told me he knew if his grandmother had been there, he would have never met that man who introduced him to Christ. And ever since he had been walking with the Lord. By the time we had reached his destination, the rider got out my car, but then stuck his head back in the door and said, "The Lord had one question to ask you: when are you going to walk into your calling of being an evangelist?" I thought, man, get out my car. I just sat there. Then mister man shut my car door and went on his merry way.

Modeling

Who becomes a professional model at my age? I have always loved clothes, makeup, jewelry and Lord, SHOES! Modeling actually found me. On a regular, I would have never sought out to be a model because I wasn't skinny. But unbeknownst to me, the industry was changing. There were models now my age and full-figured, gorgeous women tearing up the runway.

Looking over my life, fashion and the arts has always been inside of me. I had forgotten that I had modeled twice as a little girl, and then I modeled again as an adult. Learnt the routine in one night. Then I had also forgotten that I once wanted to be an interior decorator. Some type of art always knocked at my door.

Over a period of time, I was approached twice about modeling, but I turned the person down. The third time, I remembered that I once wanted to model. I never mentioned it to anyone. I figured my opportunity to model was impossible. I wondered if this was one of my unspoken desires that God was opening a door for. I then told myself to denounce fear, and I accepted the challenge. I was sitting under an open Heaven leading me to other modeling opportunities. Second wind. I later discovered that the modeling was an avenue to me being a motivator and an encourager.

I enjoy and feel honored to meet designers and sport their clothing. Meeting designers and models for dinner and kicking it with them is a pleasure. It was told to me by a designer that I bring their designs to life. Supportive relationships have been birthed out of some of these connections. Whoever would have thought that I would be on this fashion journey? I have even been interviewed to take part in a fashion documentary that will be previewed in the 69th Street Movie Theater in May 2020.

During my first conversation over the phone with my new modeling coach, she said "I have one question...why purple?" I laughed out loud. She was referring to my purple hair color.

Everyone should find the niche of how to share their talents, gifts, and personality with others. No man or woman should be an island. Everyone needs someone. Our fallen world needs us all to pick each other up. I am finding avenues to bring empowerment, encouragement, confidence, and assurance through my smile, words, and performances on the runway. I am able to draw people in and get their attention with my smile, character, humor and with my purple hair.

Living to Live Again: Second Wind

I am free, praise the Lord, I'm free. No longer bound. No more chains holding me. My soul is resting. It's such a blessing. Praise the Lord, hallelujah, I'm free. And being free is an attachment to peace of mind, thinking about peace, and absorbing a life of peace.

Many times, when you tap into your life there are incidents that just may stand out more than others. Incidents that have happened that you cannot change. But you can decide to march on. I am really a unique individual who became able to embrace being different. I see most of my incidents as lessons. What did I need to learn? I needed to learn how to live. How to maneuver through the difficult ups and downs. How to be strong and resilient. Life does so much to us. Yet, if we watch and listen carefully, life is also a teacher. So many dreams have flowed through this hemisphere that has attached themselves to me. Experiences of births, a miscarriage, car accidents, surgeries, falls, illnesses, deaths, and financial ruins. I have had three sleep tests. The sleep specialist said I don't get enough sleep. (Like I don't know that. I've been a night hawk since I was a child. My mother can vouch for that.) Yet a lesson I am learning is to rest in the arms of Jesus and to breathe with purpose.

God wakes me up every morning. New mercies I see every day. In the midst of so much turmoil, God is still blessing me.

The beat goes on.

CONFIDENCE

The word "confidence" affects everyone in this world. Either you have it, or you don't. How does an individual wear their focus of **Confidence?**

The word **Confidence** means complete or full trust in something or someone. In other words, there is no doubt. There is no second-guessing.

Having **Confidence** can be a gift you give to yourself. Having **Confidence** can be a vehicle to open doors for success in life. That works by believing in yourself that you have the ability to make a task happen. Anyone who has **Confidence** in themselves is unstoppable. When you are unstoppable, you are resilient. You keep pushing forward no matter what anyone says or does. You have the confidence, and you believe in yourself. To have **Confidence** is a gift and a prize.

Once a baby's legs are strong enough to stand, it has **Confidence** in itself to let go of an adult's hand to move forward and walk on a sure foundation.

Confidence can also be stolen from someone by another's words that are spoken or how someone is treated by another. Many times, this type of theft will bruise a person's self-esteem. It robs an individual of their character.

Note: Negative words spoken over a child early in life will plant seeds in their mind and in their emotions that they are not good enough. A person will feel unloved by others. Plus, more than likely, they will not even love themselves. That is one example of why individuals cut, self-inflict themselves— because they have inner rage and pain.

*Name-calling or telling someone they will never be important beats at an individual's self-esteem, causing a person to lack **Confidence**. **This is a negative action**, and if done enough, it will cause a person to question if they are important. Sticks and stones do break bones, and name-calling does hurt.*

For example, after being molested or abused, a person may believe that they are worthless. They are stripped of their dignity. When anyone steps over anyone's boundaries, that is penetrating disrespect on another being. Then depression can seep into their emotions. When a person lacks **Confidence**, they may act out from a hurt place. An individual may turn to illicit sexual activity, negative relationships, drinking, drugs, or wild partying to fill a void, or they may commit suicide.

Anyone who suffers with lack of **Confidence** may possibly deal with fear or feel rejected.

Fear is the opposite of **Confidence**. Remember the Lion in *The Wizard of Oz?* He lacked courage. As big as he was, the Lion was afraid of little dog Toto. His lack of courage held him back until he got courage. Fear will stifle someone, causing them to be stagnant. Fear will keep an individual bound from receiving their blessings and keep them stuck in a mental dark place, away from moving forward toward great things and success in life.

That is not God's way. Jesus wants us to have life and to have life abundantly. The Lord wants us to have **Confidence** in ourselves. The Lord wants you to stand up strong within yourself. He wants you to build strong legs and strong muscles so that you may walk on a sure foundation. Jesus wants us to dream and reach for the sky. The Lord believes in you. He believes in you so much that he has set a table for you to devour. Taste and see that the Lord is good. Umm, umm good. God gave us all talents and gifts for a reason. They were given to use. God is not okay with fear and self-esteem issues to be placed inside of us. God does not give us fear. He gave us a sound mind. God gave us stability. And we can go to Jesus our shepherd and our mediator to ask for assistance with obtaining **Confidence**. God wants us to live to our full potential. God wants you to be successful.

Confidence has a voice. **Confidence** can speak soft. Or **Confidence** can speak loudly. But the most effective **Confident** voice is the **Confident** voice that speaks clearly and understandably.

How does someone obtain **Confidence?**

Assurance and belief. Affirm yourself by speaking words of **Confidence** to yourself. Write yourself notes. I am the head. I am fearfully and wonderfully made. I am a gift. I can do all things that strengthens me. I am more than a conqueror through Jesus Christ. Whatever negative energy that has been spoken into your life, affirm the opposite.

I am lovable.

I am loved.

I am beautiful.

I am handsome.

I am brilliant.

I AM SUCCESSFUL!

Affirmations bring a positive mindset and can brighten atmospheres. Affirmations speak and bring joy to a person's life. Affirmations bring confidence and belief when spoken out loud and thought inside of the mind. Speak positive affirmations to yourself continually from your own tongue: I think I can. I know I can. I believe I can. I know I will birth confidence inside myself.

How do you maintain **Confidence?**

By praying and meditating.

Praying is talking to God. Converse with God about who you are. Ask God how to be strategic about your life. Your words to God don't have to be pretty. They just should be real about your circumstance. Share with the Lord where you are. If you feel weak, admit that, and ask God to give you strength.

Use meditation time to reflect and speak to yourself on behalf of yourself. Affirm that you are awesome. Affirm that you have a wonderful, incredible life regardless of any circumstance.

Let's put a plug in right here. Be optimistic about your confidence-building journey.

Optimism means to have expectations for a favorable outcome. When we are thinking about outcome, we are focusing on the end product. The equation for outcome is coming out. You are coming out of thinking dark into thinking into the MARVELOUS light. Your journey is a process.

Think about what you desire to be. Do whatever you desire to accomplish. Go wherever you desire to travel or move. Whenever someone goes on a trip, they generally pack a bag or a suitcase. They put inside the bag essentials that will be needed on their trip. They also pack for what they will need once they get to their destination. Not to mention once they arrive, they may still need to pick up some type of essential once they arrive.

Make plans and set goals and follow through with your goals. Take baby steps if you have to. Every time you accomplishment something, celebrate yourself. Watch your confidence in yourself grow.

Get around positive people and positive influences. Those that support you. Those that encourage you. Those that see the glass half-full. Whoever doesn't, they aren't the right person to be around.

Cherish your **Confidence.** Just like beauty is in the beholder. **Confidence** is a beautiful accessory. Wear it like a diamond.

When we build our foundation on Christ, there is nothing that we cannot do nor is there anything we cannot become when we believe and have **Confidence** in ourselves. If you have faith the size of a mustard seed and work at your **Confidence**, you can accomplish anything. Yes, it takes work. Put on your big people undies and pull them up by its elastic. You can build your **Confidence** in you. Fight for yourself. Yes, you can. I believe in YOU!

THE BENEDICTION

After losing a young lady who was very instrumental in Vision Productions Inc., God reiterated to me while sitting at her homegoing service that my work planting seeds is important enough for me to continue moving forward. I am a seed planter in the Earth.

Life is so precious. It's something that many take for granted. When I got the call that Erica's life had been snuffed out of her, I just sat in the car at Wawa for hours. I sat there in shock. It was hard to grasp what was said over the phone. It took me two hours to drive home when it should have taken 20 minutes. I have never driven that slow in my life. I prayed that this was a mistake. Obviously, it was not a mistake being we were sitting at her homegoing service saying our final goodbyes.

Don't waste time. Don't waste your life.

ABOUT THE AUTHOR

Ms. Lynda Joice is the mother to Dr. Taressa J. Sanders and Minister Professor Mack D. Sanders. She is also an anti-bullying advocate, a producer, a visionary, an entrepreneur, a published author, a playwright, a certified nurse's assistant, a certified computer programmer/operator, a certified sound and video technician, a Lyft driver, and a retired educator. She has been an actress and a sound, video, and lighting assistant for services, plays, and weddings. Lynda loves to read and has a private home library owning over 300 books. Being in God's will is a major goal of Lynda's. She loves the Lord, her family, music, taking pictures, writing, and reading. Lynda's dad was her first musical inspiration as a leader of his own singing group, the Gospel Five. Lynda has sang on numerous church and school choirs including Wagner Alumni and Philadelphia Mass Youth Choir. She began studying piano at the age of eleven under the teachings of first Vera Eubanks and then Professor Charles Pettiway. For a period of time, Lynda also taught elementary piano at Eva Donaldson's Music School.

Lynda began directing youth and adult choirs as a teenager and became the youngest paid director for the Christlike PG. Faith Baptist Church. Lynda held that position for over 10 years. Some years later, she assisted directing the Senior Choir and the ECM Choir of Mt. Airy COGIC.

Lynda has coordinated after school programs, youth events, graduations, assemblies, glee clubs, youth concerts, and talent shows. She also served for several years as a summer camp counselor. Lynda later received her Arts/Education degree in 2014.

Lynda's company, the Vision Productions Inc. is a positive haven where young and seasoned adults can channel and showcase their artistic talents and gifts in playwrighting, photography, videography, singing, theater, dance, music, and other visual arts. A portion of VISION's endeavors is to build confidence and empower individuals. The production company was also created to give a safe environment where individuals use their abilities to reach those who thirst spiritually, emotionally, and mentally. The productions that are performed are modern day, real life, and practical situations. The company often operates out of love and unity. In the past, her company has spearheaded clothing drives, skating and bowling parties, and anti-bullying events.

To add to her literary list, Lynda is a published author of two book collaborations, *What is a Courageous Woman* and *Stiletto Stand Diaries*. *Surviving on Broken Pieces* will be her first solo published project.

A major mission in Lynda's life is to keep learning how to help empower others, especially the youth so they may excel and reach their full potentials. One of her greatest passions is to help those who are hurting. She believes if hurt is not healed properly it can ruin a prominent future and someone's life. She is determined to use her talents, gifts, knowledge, and experiences to make a difference. Her brand is advocating for youth and productions.

Made in the USA
Middletown, DE
04 May 2021